Masquerade: The Amazing Camouflage Deceptions of
World War II
The Day They Stole the Mona Lisa

The Day
They Stole
the Mona Lisa

———

Seymour V. Reit

SUMMIT BOOKS / NEW YORK

10 9 8 7 6 5 4 3 2 1

Library of Congress Cataloging in Publication Data

Reit, Seymour.
    The day they stole the Mona Lisa.

    Includes bibliographical references and index.
    1   Leonardo da Vinci, 1452–1519.   Mona Lisa.
2. Art thefts.   I.   Title.
ND623.L5A7   1981   364.1'62'0944361   80–22297
ISBN 0–671–25056–6

Acknowledgments

Many people were generous with their time and effort in helping me to put together the pieces of this puzzle.

I wish to thank all for their kind assistance—in particular, Phoebe Peebles and Agnes Mongan of the Fogg Art Museum, Boston; Bonnie Burnham of the I.F.A.R., New York; Gregory Hedberg of the Minneapolis Institute of Arts; Suzanne Zolper of the Walters Art Gallery, Baltimore; Alan P. Darr of the Detroit Institute of Arts; Phyllis A. Gray of the Bass Art Museum, Miami Beach; Susan H. Norris of the Carnegie Institute, Pittsburgh; Sona Johnston of the Baltimore Museum of Art; and Rupert Hodge of the Witt Library, Courtauld Institute, London.

Additional thanks go to Patrick Conan of the Metropolitan Museum of Art Research Library, Oscar Krasner of New York's Krasner Gallery, Betty and Michael Varese, Milton Esterow, Teresa Van Wemmel, Marco Grassi, Suzanne Swick and Thomas J. Hubbard; also to the staff of the microfilm room of the New York Public Library.

For their help in France, I am indebted to M. Roger Couterel of the Paris Prefecture of Police, to Madeleine Hours and Lola Faillant-Dumas of the Musée du Louvre, and to Mlle. Laurence Marceillac of the museum's Service d'Étude et de Documentation. Thanks are due also to Patrice Hekking of Nice, for his time and cooperation. A special word of deep appreciation goes to journalist Jeffrey Robinson of St.-Laurent-du-Var, whose diligence and enthusiasm opened many stubborn doors to me in France, and whose advice and assistance were most greatly valued. For help with the Italian side of this narrative, my thanks go to Cavaliere Silio Sensi of the Uffizi Gallery, to Carlo Mansuino of Florence's Biblioteca Nazionale, and to writer-editor Ronald Strom, of Rome.

Sincere appreciation goes also to my superb translator, Grace Myra Jackman; and, for additional translations, to Renée Schaff and Ellen Lask. And finally, many thanks to my typist Diane Lewis, who worked so competently on the various drafts and changes.

For Edmée

Contents

Picture section follows page 160

Foreword

A hundred years ago, French historian Jules Michelet wrote of the *Mona Lisa*, "This painting entices me, calls me, usurps me, absorbs me; I go to it in spite of myself, as the bird goes to the serpent."

For generations, countless art lovers have been similarly enticed, called, usurped, absorbed. In Paris in the early 1900s, one of these was an elegant gentleman of impeccable dress and manner; and the spell cast on him by the famous portrait was so intense that he decided to do something extraordinary.

This is the story, the true story, of what he did and how he did it—a history of creative knavery on a scale which in the art world has never been equaled. The narrative may read like detective fiction, but it decidedly isn't. Everything described in these pages happened: the people are real people; so, too, are the names, places, dates, times and events. Much of the dialogue also comes directly from official documents, news reports, letters and personal recollections. In some instances dialogue and soliloquy have had to be reconstructed, to add human dimension and advance the narrative; but such liberties have been kept to a minimum, and are fully consistent with what is known of the principals and their activities.

Collecting the assorted pieces of this jigsaw puzzle took several years of research which carried me to Paris, Nice, Florence and Rome. In the United States it entailed numerous interviews and contacts with dealers, gallery owners, museum curators and art professionals scattered from Boston to Miami, from Baltimore to Houston to San Diego.

Surprisingly, the details of this baroque escapade aren't widely known, nor have all of them ever been properly documented. Stray bits and pieces of the puzzle surface at times,

11

and a few good if brief accounts of the actual theft have appeared as part of generalized histories; but never has a major art crime caused so much turmoil when it happened, and been so widely neglected afterward. It's time now to rescue the incredible story of the *Mona Lisa* caper from limbo.

SEYMOUR V. REIT

New York, May 1980

The Mona Lisa *is without doubt the most famous painting in the world. . . . Attractive and impenetrable, with a smile set in no classifiable expression, her gaze at once magnetic but which holds no promise, she is easily characterized as the incarnation of the tenderly affectionate yet glacial "Eternal Female." And poets have often, in talking of her, made reference to the Sphinx and its enigma.*

—RENÉ HUYGHE,
Académie Française, 1974

If I had the Sistine Chapel, I could sell it tomorrow half a dozen times over.

—SIR JOSEPH DUVEEN,
art dealer

PART ONE

———

The Robbery

Steal the Mona Lisa? You might just as
well pretend that one could steal the towers
of the Cathedral of Notre-Dame.

—THÉOPHILE HOMOLLE,
director of France's
national museums

1

EARLY ON THE MORNING of August 22, 1911, an artist named Louis Beroud hurried toward the Musée du Louvre, a paint box and folding easel in one hand and an unfinished canvas in its wooden carrier in the other.

From his shabby clothes and somewhat underfed look it was evident that the young artist was "struggling," and in Paris at that time he had many counterparts. Some of his threadbare acquaintances such as Braque, Utrillo, Dufy, Modigliani and a wild Catalan named Picasso, would go on later to win considerable fame and success. Unfortunately for Beroud he wasn't destined to climb those heights, nor would he ever be acclaimed by the critics; but on that particular morning he would earn a footnote in the annals of a startling crime that was to rock the foundations of the greatest art museum in the world—not to mention the Paris Prefecture of Police, the Sûreté Nationale, and the mighty French government itself.

Beroud, unaware of all this, was engrossed in his immediate plans. As he started across the Pont Royal, the bronze hands of the huge clock on the Gare d'Orsay nudged 9 A.M. and he quickened his steps; he wanted to get to the Louvre early and start work before the crowds began filtering in. Lately he'd been having good luck; Philippe, the gallery owner, had sold several of his paintings and was waiting for more.

"I'll take all the pictures you can give me," Philippe

had said, "but I need them soon, before the season ends. When the tourists go home the money goes home."

Well, Beroud expected to finish another canvas this morning, and was glad now that he'd kept his gear with him instead of leaving it at the museum. Having a store-room in the Louvre was helpful, but the attendants, those *maladroits*, took forever to deliver equipment to the differ-ent artists and copyists; they usually got it all mixed up anyway, and today he had no time to waste.

As he crossed the bridge a cool breeze drifted over the Seine, adding to his euphoria. Paris, that summer of 1911, had been a gigantic oven; temperatures in the daytime crept into the nineties, and on August 9 in the Parc St.-Maur the thermometer had hit ninety-seven degrees. Scores of shops had closed down, the Bureau de Poste had cut mail deliveries to twice a day, and attempts were made to pump water from the Marne, duly purified, into the city's reservoirs. Parisians everywhere sweltered in the heat, sipped iced drinks, fanned themselves energetically, mopped their brows, cursed the glaring sun and enjoyed the whole drama with fine Gallic zest.

Thousands, of course, had fled to the cooler suburbs, but those who remained still had distractions. The Opéra kept bravely to its schedules; so did the Comédie Français, the Palais-Royal, Le Châtelet, the Grand-Guignol and the lively music halls of the Champs-Elysées. Military bands, their musicians parboiling in high-collared uniforms, gave nightly concerts in the public gardens; and on August 13 the firemen held their annual fair and gymnastics display at the Tuileries.

Beroud, along with half of Paris, had found relief from the heat by going swimming—highly popular that season. The municipal pools at the Place Hébert, the Rue Rouvet and the Avenue Ledru-Rollin drew big crowds for a small fee: twenty centimes for gentlemen and forty centimes for ladies, towel and bathing costume included.

For the well-to-do there were the elegant Lutétia baths, where women wore daring suits which left shoulders bare and exposed their legs up to their knees. To guard fair skin against tanning (suitable only for men) the ladies dabbed themselves with their favorite cream, *lanoline oxygenée*.

Later in August the heat wave faded, restoring Paris routines and tempers to more or less normal; and Louis, like everyone in the city, welcomed the change. Now as he hurried toward the Louvre he was tempted to linger in the bracing Seine air, but he thought of the anxious Philippe and kept going. Today he would paint; tomorrow he'd have time to relax.

From the bridge, he cut through the clutter of traffic on the embankment, narrowly missed being hit by a horse-drawn cab, and exchanged a flood of epithets with the indignant coachman. Renewed by this ritual, he hurried through the portico and went upstairs to the first floor, past the Grande Galerie and into the luminous Salon Carré. Beroud's notion of painting views of the museum's interiors had turned out well; almost anyone could make copies of Louvre masterpieces—there was a fair market for those—but scenes of the rooms themselves with all their treasures, that was something unique. Philippe had been pleased and, more important, had found buyers.

In the Salon Carré, the artist set up his canvas and arranged the colors on his palette. At the other end of the hall Mme. Aulet was already laboring over her pathetic version of the Poussin self-portrait. Louis shook his head. The dotty old creature had been copying that one painting for months; it was fast becoming her life's work. Poor Poussin—Mme. Aulet had found a lover at last. But no matter; he had already included her in his scene and had also added a few tourists, which gave the composition a nice human touch.

The Carré had always been Beroud's favorite. For

him, this gallery with its lofty ceiling and graceful propor-
tions was a codex of French history. Here, when the
Louvre was a royal palace, the Bourbons had reigned, and
Richelieu and Mazarin had contrived their plots. Before
Versailles, the Sun King had walked these floors in his
red-heeled pumps; and a hundred years ago in this very
room the Emperor Napoleon, desperate for a male heir,
had married Marie Louise of Austria. But now the princes
were gone, the palace was a museum, and the Carré
glowed with Old Masters. Louis ran an eye over the paintings displayed behind a low railing—the superb Raphaels,
the Venetian portraits, Veronese's majestic *Marriage at
Cana* which dominated the far wall . . .

He swore under his breath. Between Correggio's
Betrothal of Saint Catherine and the Titian *Allegory*, a
picture was missing—four empty hooks and a rectangular
outline stood out on the wall like a vulgar gap in a row
of flawless teeth.

A museum guard came shuffling by, his ancient uniform sagging from an equally decrepit frame, and Beroud
hurried over to him.

"Poupardin," he demanded, "where's *La Joconde?*"

Without breaking his stride, in fear perhaps that he
might never get moving again, the elderly guard shrugged
and jerked his thumb upward.

"In the studio, where else would it be? They're photo-
graphing her this morning."

Beroud's heart sank with his spirits. Why did they
have to pick the *Mona Lisa,* and this morning of all times?
Ever since that idiotic camera studio was installed, things
like this kept happening. Nothing stayed put. There were
no standards anymore, no values. Photographers in the
Louvre—*exécrable!*

His euphoria gone, the painter turned to his easel and
picked up his brushes; not that there was much he could do
until the Leonardo was back on the north wall. He had

saved that for last—that was to be his dessert—and now
he'd have to be patient and mark time. Halfheartedly he
added a dab of red to Mme. Aulet's flowered hat, wiped it
off, put it in again. He reworked a bit of the sculptured
ceiling, fussed with the perspective on his floor line, ac-
cented the gilding on several picture frames. While he
fumed and waited, a sullen half hour went by. An hour.
Still no painting.

Now it was almost eleven o'clock and tourists were
beginning to flow into the hall, stopping to study, examine,
consult their various guidebooks. Several came over to
Louis to complain (in languages he didn't understand,
though the meanings were clear enough) about the missing
portrait—the very one which all of them had particularly
wanted to see. As if its absence were *his* fault!

The artist looked at his watch, lost what patience he
had left, and went searching for Poupardin. He found the
old man dozing on a wooden stool outside the lavatory
and pushed a two-franc tip into his skinny hand.

"Listen," he cajoled, "would you find out what's
taking them so long up there? I have a picture to finish.
Be a friend; go ask them to hurry it along. Tell them it's
very important."

With a sigh Poupardin pocketed the coins and
shuffled grudgingly toward the service stairs; and, feeling
somewhat calmer, Beroud walked back to the Carré. The
tip had been extravagant, but it would get results. A little
efficiency, that's all that was needed. If he didn't shake
them up, he could be trapped here all day. The hall was
now filling with people, but he tried not to let it bother
him. As soon as they brought the madonna back he would
work quickly, finish the missing area, and take his canvas
home to dry.

Minutes later, Poupardin reappeared in the doorway
and hurried toward Beroud with odd jerky steps, his eyes
bulging. Louis looked at him curiously.

"What did they say?"

Poupardin swallowed and managed a hoarse whisper. *"La Joconde* isn't there. It hasn't been there at all. The photographers know nothing about it."

Beroud stared at him uncomprehending. What did he mean, not there? What was the old fool mumbling about? It couldn't be a joke—not from the look on his face.

The unhappy guard repeated his litany. *"La Joconde* is gone—disappeared!"

With an effort, Louis gathered his thoughts. Poupardin wasn't making any sense. Paintings didn't just vanish, not from a museum like the Louvre. Surely if they'd taken the *Mona Lisa* away to clean or to reframe, the guard would have known about it; so the picture *had* to be in the photo studio; that was the only logical explanation. Or was it?

Outside, on the busy avenues flanking the museum, the morning traffic quickened its pace. Coaches, wagons and motorbuses jousted noisily with each other, and all of them bullied the peddlers guiding their pushcarts slowly along the curbs. Behind the Louvre in the green gardens of the Tuileries, children played games and sailed their toy boats in the octagonal basin, while older people sauntered along the gravel paths under the chestnut trees, enjoying the amiable weather.

But inside the Salon Carré, for Beroud and Poupardin, the world had come to a sudden halt.

"C'est parti!" repeated the guard, his face tense with anxiety.

For a long frozen moment, oblivious to the other visitors, they turned and looked again as if hoping it had all been a mistake. There was the wall with its taunting hooks and the bare outline of the missing masterpiece. As Louis watched, the hooks turned to fangs and the violated space seemed to expand, growing larger and larger until it swallowed the room in a strange feral emptiness.

Where was the *Mona Lisa?*

What had happened to the Louvre's most famous painting?

Wrenching himself from his trance, Poupardin lurched off on ancient legs to report this crisis to the chief of guards, while the young artist went on staring at the wall, hypnotized. Louis Beroud was so stunned he forgot all about the two francs he had wasted on Poupardin.

2

ON SUNDAY the twentieth, two days before the disappearance of the *Mona Lisa,* Georges Picquet stomped through the Louvre's upper galleries, yawning heavily. A big lunch had made him sleepy and he would have enjoyed a quiet nap downstairs, but it was out of the question. Sunday, especially in the holiday months, was a busy period and there was too much for him to do.

Picquet, head of the museum's custodial staff, leaned his vast bulk against a marble balustrade and surveyed the crowds with a baleful eye as they streamed up the stairways and into the great halls. They were the usual cross section: local Parisians, young disciples from the Academy and the Sorbonne, teachers and art connoisseurs, families from the provinces dressed in their Sunday best, Dutch and Spanish tour groups, rich Americans and dour Scandinavians, voluble Italians, busloads of stolid Germans, a scattering of colonials from North Africa, and brisk English ladies with Baedekers in hand, determined to make the most of every cultural moment.

Despite the diversity of these pilgrims, Georges Picquet managed to resent all of them with equal impartiality; nonetheless they came to his domain in great numbers.

In those years the Louvre was, as today, one of the

marvels of Paris. Along with the Arc de Triomphe, Notre-
Dame, the Champs-Elysées, Napoleon's tomb in the
Invalides and Alexandre Eiffel's spectacular tower, the
famous building drew hordes of visitors—some four or five
thousand every day. The *Guide Michelin* called it "the
largest palace in the world," and in the words of art
historian Milton S. Fox, "It is not enough to say that the
Louvre is the richest of museums, a vast treasury of arts
and civilizations, magnificently housed. It has a deeper
meaning. The Louvre is a living idea."

The roots of that idea go back to the thirteenth century when Philip Augustus, the warrior king, built a feudal
fortress on this spot to protect his growing town of Paris.
Three hundred years later, King Francis I had a new palace
built on the ancient Capetian ruins, some of which can
still be seen in the museum's cellars. It was this same ruler
who became Leonardo da Vinci's patron during the
genius's final years. At that time, Francis I also obtained
from Leonardo what we have come to regard as the
legendary *Mona Lisa*.

Here in his elegant Pavillon du Roi, Francis assembled the great Renaissance art masterpieces which formed
the basis of the Louvre's collections. Other monarchs,
Henri II, his wife Catherine de' Medici, Henri IV, Louis
XIII and Louis XIV rebuilt and enlarged the palace and
added to its treasures. In the wake of the French Revolution
royal palaces became superfluous, and in 1793 the Louvre
was officially named a National Museum of the Arts. Later
it was further enriched and expanded by Bonaparte and
Napoleon III.

In the course of its life the great edifice had been
neglected, damaged, plundered and defaced. After Louis
XIV moved his court to Versailles, it was taken over by
squatters. During the Revolution it was used as an arsenal,
and in 1871 it was set on fire by fanatical Communards.
But it survived all of history's assaults, and by 1911 Georges

Picquet's marble realm was accepted everywhere as the greatest, most prestigious art center in the world.

The Louvre, which has continued to grow, then housed over 275,000 separate items. The paintings on its walls included fifty-four Rubens, twenty-two Rembrandts, sixteen Titians and more Spanish masterpieces than in any gallery outside Spain. Its Greek and Roman sculptures numbered in the thousands, among them the famous *Venus de Milo* and the *Victory of Samothrace*. Over the years these displays were enhanced by contributions from such wealthy patrons as the Lallemants, the Vandeuls, the Rothschilds and the de Morgans.

In addition to paintings and sculpture, the building housed vast collections of antique pottery, ancient bronzes and ornaments, medieval and Renaissance tapestries, rare ivories and *objets d'art,* fifty thousand priceless drawings, fine furniture of the seventeenth and eighteenth centuries, an Asiatic Museum, an Egyptian Museum, a Chinese Museum, a Museum of Decorative Arts and, surprisingly, a Marine Museum devoted to early shipbuilding and navigation. All of this was spread out over forty-five acres of elegant galleries—an area three times larger than the Vatican, including the Basilica of St. Peter. The Picture Gallery alone was three hundred yards long and carried more antique frames on its walls than could be found in any other museum.

In terms of size, it has been estimated that it would take a person two full hours to walk through the Louvre, without stopping anywhere.

Georges Picquet, the head custodian, was perhaps one of the few people who had ever made that extensive tour. Now, as he leaned on the balustrade on August 20, 1911, he watched the crowds and sighed unhappily. Picquet the xenophobe felt protective toward his world; to him, most of these visitors were *salauds*—thoughtless boors who

trampled his beautiful floors, smudged his walls, pawed the
sculptures, damaged the displays and left an endless trail
of lost umbrellas, books, packages and gloves behind.

Affronted by the mere thought of it all, he turned
from the stairwell and continued his rounds. Two more
hours and his martyrdom would be over, at least for a
little while. On Mondays the museum was closed to the
general public. It was the time traditionally set aside for
cleaning, repairs, rearranging exhibits—*his* day, when he
could take charge and get things tidied up properly.

The bored custodian crossed the Chinese Gallery and
yawned again. Only two hours until closing. It had been,
all in all, an ordinary Sunday: quiet, uneventful, no different from hundreds he'd been through before. And those
types wandering around his halls like so many glassy-eyed
sheep—they were dull, too. Dull, faceless, uninteresting;
the Louvre's Sunday visitors were all alike.

But for once Picquet was mistaken.

3

AT 2:45 THAT AFTERNOON, short, stocky Vincenzo Perugia,
looking every inch the average visitor in his straw hat and
rusty black suit, strolled through the museum entrance at
the Porte Denon. Blending with the crowd, he headed for
the Escalier Daru and climbed one flight to the Picture
Gallery, gently pressing his elbow against the slight bulge
under his jacket.

Sometime earlier, Perugia had been employed as a
workman in the building; now he hoped nervously that
he wouldn't run into any familiar faces. But he was prepared for that, the *signore* had coached him well. If he met
someone he knew, he would remain calm and casual; a few
friendly words together and that would be that. After all,

as the *signore* had pointed out, it was a normal thing to visit the Louvre—what better way to pass a few hours on a Sunday? Still, he hoped it wouldn't be necessary to speak to anyone; it might cause problems later.

Perugia reached inside his jacket and made sure that the hidden bundle was still there.

At about the same time, using the gate at the Pavillon Sully, the Lancelotti brothers, Vincent and Michele, entered the museum, went upstairs and strolled past the Watteaus and Bouchers in the Salle La Caze. Attempting to look commonplace—in their case hardly difficult—the Lancelottis were also dressed inconspicuously. Vincent wore his only suit (dark brown), a white shirt (reasonably clean) and a plain blue tie (borrowed for the occasion). Michele had on a new tweed cap and under his nondescript jacket a gray turtleneck sweater. For an added touch of tourist realism, he carried a bulky folding camera on a strap. The camera, acquired at a pawnshop in Belleville, was an affectation he would later regret.

Shortly before 3 P.M., Perugia and the Lancelottis came into a small gallery called the Salle Duchatel. Here, under Meynier's elegant painted ceiling, they exchanged glances and sauntered self-consciously past the Ingres portraits and Luini frescoes. The vibrant colors of these masterpieces electrified the room, but the three men were unaware of it. Vincenzo Perugia glanced at his watch. Just one hour until closing time; with a little luck, it would be enough.

The stocky man in the straw hat was simple, uneducated, and not very bright. Years later a court psychiatrist would even characterize him as "intellectually deficient." Yet he had a degree of natural shrewdness which would come in handy, and he had been chosen for this assignment for a most plausible reason.

Eleven months earlier, in October 1910, the directors of the Louvre had come to a painful decision. At that time there were serious problems—a valuable painting had been splashed with acid by a viewer who "disapproved" of it, and a lunatic had slashed at another canvas with a knife. Vandalism was and still is a continuing nightmare to curators of priceless art. In 1910, afraid of repetitions, the museum officials decided to put some of their treasures, including the *Mona Lisa,* under protective glass.

The French art community had been scandalized, and protests came thick and fast. Glass coverings? *Quel blasphème!* The reflections, said the purists, would cut down visibility and ruin the paintings' subtle effects. But Théophile Homolle, France's director of national museums, ignored the outcry and called in a Paris firm of carpenters and glaziers, M. Corbier Compagnie, to handle the much-needed project.

For the da Vinci portrait the contractors designed a shadow box large enough to house the painting plus its ornate frame, and fitted into this was a thick pane of glass. Putting it all together was a complex process, and the device had to be built and rebuilt several times before M. Homolle gave his final approval. But the *Mona Lisa* was penned in at last, the workmen thanked and dismissed—and the worried Louvre directors, surveying the results, breathed sighs of relief at a possible disaster averted.

The Paris contracting firm had assigned four experienced men to build the glass case for the *Mona Lisa.* One member of this team was a young Italian carpenter named Vincenzo Perugia.

Now, in the Salle Duchatel on that crucial Sunday, Perugia and the Lancelottis hovered near a radial stand that held drawings by Renaissance masters. The men were seemingly absorbed in the display, but Perugia kept an eye on the room's two archways. One led to a foyer shop where photographs, etchings and art books were sold. The other opened directly into the larger Salon Carré. The

Duchatel itself was one of the museum's less frequented galleries. A popular guidebook of the period noted that for new visitors it was "advisable to traverse the Salle Duchatel without stopping," and to begin their serious viewing elsewhere. So at times the room, even on busy days, stood momentarily empty, and there were no guards stationed nearby.

While the three men waited anxiously, people drifted in and out of the gallery, which had been named for its benefactor, the Comtesse Duchatel. Visitors came and went in an exasperatingly steady stream, but by 3:20 P.M. only one young couple remained in the hall with Perugia and his helpers. Minutes later, as the young people sauntered out to the photo shop, the three men were grouped around a large Bramantino painting, examining it intently. They were considerably less interested in the Bramantino than in a small storage room located directly behind it.

The weeks in which Perugia worked on the glass case had been profitable for him in more ways than one. In and out of the building at all hours, particularly on Mondays, he had learned (and remembered) a great deal about the Louvre's inner rhythms. He came to know the patterns of the crowds, the schedules of the guards, the locations of the service entrances, which doors would admit him freely and which were kept locked. He also knew about the storeroom behind the Salle Duchatel.

The Louvre, like many museums, had always allowed students, teachers and hobbyists freedom to sketch and paint in certain galleries, the only hard and fast rule being that they couldn't duplicate any work of art in its correct dimensions; to guard against possible forgery, no masterpiece could be copied in the same size as the original, though smaller and larger versions were permitted. As an added service, the museum also provided a place where copyists' easels, camp chairs, unfinished canvases and bits

of sculpture could be stored overnight. Attendants collected these items at closing time and distributed them to
the artists on the following day or when requested.

The place where this equipment was kept was a narrow
chamber behind the east wall of the Duchatel. To preserve
the appearance of this wall, the storeroom had an artfully
designed *trompe l'oeil* door. Vincenzo Perugia not only was
familiar with this door, but knew how to spring the concealed latch.

Because of the large numbers of visitors, no artists
were allowed to work in the museum on Sundays; and on
Mondays, of course, the Louvre wasn't open to the public.
This meant that *from closing time on Sunday until Tuesday morning* nobody would have any reason to use or enter
the storeroom. Perugia also knew that, given the museum's
lax security arrangements, watchmen rarely if ever poked
their heads into this little area.

At 3:45 P.M., fifteen minutes before Sunday closing,
guards at the entrances began turning new visitors away
from the museum. Meanwhile, other guards and attendants
set out on their customary sweep through the halls and
galleries, patiently guiding sightseers toward the various
exits and announcing, *"On ferme!"* The custodian,
Georges Picquet, came downstairs and took up his ritual
post at the foot of the Escalier Henri II, where the day's
crop of lost articles would be assembled and sorted. Pleased
that his duties would shortly be over, he watched the
visitors streaming toward the exits.

By 4:10 P.M. the day's multitudes had finally vacated
the huge colonnaded building; all of Picquet's tedious
intruders were gone at last. All but three. Tucked away
in the cramped storeroom behind the Duchatel, making
themselves more or less comfortable among assorted easels,
paint boxes, sketch pads and dusty racks of unfinished
canvases, were Vincenzo Perugia and the brothers
Lancelotti.

Squatting on the floor with his back against the alcove wall, the carpenter took the bundle from beneath his jacket and placed it carefully beside him; and his companions drew similar packets from under their clothes. The men exchanged glances and Perugia nodded silently, his lips in a thin smile. *Tutto va bene;* but it was child's play—the real test would come in the morning.

4

TO THE ROSTER of history's greatest and most persuasive con-artists must now be added the name of another legendary figure, the "Marqués Eduardo de Valfierno." The elegant Marqués, as he then called himself—at times there had been other *noms de guerre*—had been born in Buenos Aires in the late 1850s, the youngest son of a wealthy *estanciero* of Castilian lineage. When this affluent landowner died, young Eduardo found himself almost penniless, since his father's fortune—the estates, rents, stables, everything—went by tradition to the eldest son.

The younger brother was left with three uninspired career alternatives: the diplomatic corps, the military or the clergy, anything else being considered improper for someone of his social standing. Since none of these options meshed in any way with his tastes or temperament, Valfierno decided to live, however precariously, by his wits and charm. But even for so casual a goal and life style, large amounts of pesos are needed. For a while Eduardo got by on nerve and promissory notes; later he began selling works of art which had been bequeathed him over the years by various family members. With his excellent connections in Buenos Aires society, it was easy enough for him to find buyers. Little by little the beautiful Sèvres porcelains, the bronzes and Oriental vases, the Tanagra

figurines, the Capo-di-Monte, the rare drawings and paintings all disappeared; and presently the walls and cabinets
in Valfierno's rooms on the Avenida de Mayo were dis-
tressingly bare.

At that point the "Marqués" apparently did some
serious thinking about survival, and his solution to the
problem was simple: since he no longer had genuine
antiques to dispose of, he would have to create and market
new ones. He also enlarged his contacts to include the
aristocrats of São Paolo and Rio de Janeiro, as well as busi-
nessmen and well-heeled tourists from the booming cities
of North America.

Those years near the turn of the century were a time
of vast tax-free fortunes easily made and readily spent—a
period, art collector James Jarves has noted, when "it had
become the mode to have taste." For many nouveau-riche
Americans, one way to acquire that taste was to buy large
amounts of it with hard cash—and Eduardo de Valfierno
was happy to accommodate them. The forging of antiqui-
ties, especially in the decorative arts, was then a thriving
business (it still is; only the geography has changed). As
one art historian wrote, "Since the middle of the 19th
century, frauds of this kind have been offered to tourists
all over the world. In France, Italy, Germany and England
industries were established to cater to the expanding demand . . . sometimes the wares were even exported to the
alleged countries of origin."

Selling taste had become big business, and the
pseudonymous Marqués's naïve clients were delighted with
the "priceless" antiques and "rare" artifacts supplied by
this urbane, cultured gentleman, who seemed not so much
an art dealer as simply a kind and helpful friend.

As Valfierno prospered he aimed for higher stakes
and soon concentrated on selling "old Spanish masters,"
particularly the works of the great Andalusian painter

Bartolomé Murillo. By that time the Marqués had joined forces with a brilliant art restorer who had come from Marseilles, one Yves Chaudron. Karl Decker, a veteran journalist and friend of Valfierno's, who later became his biographer, described this artist as "a pale wisp of a Frenchman, almost a skeleton," whose skill as a forger (under Valfierno's tutelage) was of the "uncanny sort that breaks the heart of the collector."

Yves Chaudron was a perfect balance to Valfierno. The impeccable Marqués, socially adept and at ease with people of all kinds, provided the front; Chaudron, laconic, self-effacing, gifted and industrious, supplied the talent. Between them—with the help of several close-lipped accomplices—the two con men set up a thriving "Murillo factory," turning out facsimile paintings which Valfierno firmly maintained were as good as if not superior to the master's originals. At no time was the Marqués burdened with guilt or prey to defensive feelings; quite the contrary. "Chaudron and I," he confided to Karl Decker with a touch of pride, "enriched the Argentine." He also insisted that "a forged painting so cleverly executed as to puzzle experts is as valuable an addition to the art wealth of the world as the original."

Rich South American widows, recently bereaved, became excellent prospects and bought spurious Murillos to donate to favorite churches in memory of their dear departed husbands. The inevitable tourists, in the market for quick culture, were also good customers, and Chaudron's forgeries soon found their way north to be proudly exhibited in gaudy mansions from Savannah to San Francisco. There is reason to believe that a Chaudron fake also wound up in the art collection of the Vatican. Purchased from Valfierno by a wealthy Brazilian, it was given to a member of the Spanish royal family, who then presented it to the Vatican's curators. According to the records, X rays of this "Murillo" showed that it had been painted over a work known to be from a period later than the seventeenth-century years in which Murillo lived. Chaudron, eager to find suitable old canvas for his frauds, had neglected to scrape off the underpainting—a lapse in his usual diligence; but by the time of that discovery the "Murillo factory" had long ceased to exist.

By about 1908, in spite of his success, the Marqués grew bored with South America. He also felt that the opportunities there had been largely exhausted and, looking for new challenges, shifted his base to Paris with occasional forays to London, Madrid and the Riviera. Here in Europe he continued, with his usual skill, as a purveyor of status and illusions. Yves Chaudron decided to stay behind in Buenos Aires and carry on "production," though without Valfierno's commanding presence Murillo sales declined rapidly.

Then, in the fall of 1910, the juxtaposition of two events steered the veteran toward what would be the most spectacular of his undertakings. First, he read with interest of the plan to put glass shields on some of the Louvre's masterpieces. Second, the cadaverous Chaudron, giving up at last in Buenos Aires, resurfaced in Paris and contacted his former confederate. This combination proved irresistible to Eduardo: with Chaudron's talents as a copyist and his own gifts as a salesman, all they needed to develop a viable scheme was a suitable inside man.

"He should be," the Marqués mused to Chaudron over wine at the Café Vachette, "somebody who's worked in the Louvre and knows it well; perhaps someone who had a hand in installing those glass cases."

Finding the right man was, for Valfierno, a simple enough process. A few hours spent in the dingy workmen's cafés and bistros of the Nineteenth Arrondissement, a number of guarded inquiries dropped here and there—the trail led in no time at all to the one he needed and the carpenter, Perugia, had been more than receptive.

Now, as the Marqués dressed for dinner that Sunday evening at his hotel, he fought the urge to gape stupidly at his watch. There was nothing more he could do; if everything had gone as planned, Perugia and those helpers of his were safely hidden in the storeroom. Now it was all a matter of luck, timing, the spin of the wheel.

Well, risk and riches seemed to go together; at least it had often been so in his case. Of course he wasn't content with Perugia; the man was a simpleton, but he could be shrewd at times, and his knowledge of the museum had made him a practical choice. To improve the odds, Valfierno had coached and rehearsed him endlessly. He also knew about Perugia's police record and previous arrests— facts which had helped him keep the carpenter docile and compliant.

He himself was safe enough; even if all three men were caught in the Louvre redhanded, they couldn't implicate the Marqués. There wasn't a shred of connecting evidence; they didn't know his name or where to find him, and they certainly knew nothing about his true plans for the *Mona Lisa*. All that Perugia and the Lancelottis knew was that he was an ephemeral figure who chose to be called "the *signore*." Nothing more. And if the entire plan went awry and he were somehow traced and questioned, he could still deny everything. Of course he would arrange alibis. Tonight he would dine at Ledoyen, not only with his friends but with half the *haut monde* of Paris. Tomorrow perhaps a visit to the races at Longchamp, where he could manage some unobtrusive visibility. Whatever might happen to the men in the Salle Duchatel, he personally wouldn't be in danger.

Standing before the mirror, he adjusted his meticulous

cravat, added a pearl stickpin and regarded himself with mild approval. A bit paunchy perhaps, a bit past his prime and somewhat old-fashioned; a gilded barge in an age of steam. Still, the effect was satisfactory.

Taking his hat and cloak, Valfierno stepped from his rooms and closed the door softly behind him. Everything in America was ready, and he was on the verge of his *coup de maître*—the most unusual, certainly most ambitious deception he had ever attempted. His entire future, oddly, was now in the hands of a stupid carpenter and his two dull assistants; and if the whole thing had a slight feeling of unreality it was, in a way, to be expected. The blueprint was so bizarre, so capricious, it could be followed seriously only if taken lightly.

For the first time in years Eduardo felt exhilarated and acutely alive. The next twenty-four hours would tell the tale. By this time tomorrow he would be the most disappointed man in all of Paris, or one of the wealthiest.

5

THERE WERE FOOTSTEPS outside. The three men in the storeroom looked at one another and froze, not daring to breathe. The steps approached from the photo shop, moved leisurely across the Salle Duchatel within yards of their hiding place, then receded down the long sweep of the Grande Galerie. Silence fell, and their tension eased.

Perugia brushed nervously at his large mustache and fanned himself with his hard straw hat. Michele scratched and stared into space. Vincent took a wedge of cheese from his pocket and began to munch it stoically. The carpenter watched a bit enviously, regretting now that he hadn't remembered to bring food. But with his stomach so tense, perhaps it was just as well. Later he could eat all he wanted; he would gorge himself, with plenty of expensive wine to wash it down. Faint light sifted through a grid high on the wall, and Perugia tried to read the hands on his watch; the hours were passing very slowly. The alcove smelled heavily of turpentine, paint, mildew and damp clay, and he fought back an urge to sneeze. That could be disastrous; the *signore* had mentioned over and over how important it was to keep totally silent while under cover.

For the hundredth time that week, Perugia went over his instructions. The *signore* had drilled and drilled them —the timing, the diagrams, the key for the ground-floor stairway; they had rehearsed it again and again. The man had even had a panel of wood sawed to the proper size so that they could learn to handle the da Vinci once it was out of the frame. Not that it was necessary. Didn't he, Vincenzo Perugia, know all about *La Gioconda*? Hadn't he personally worked for weeks on the shadow box? Didn't he help to build it with his own hands? The *signore* was an autocrat; he treated them like imbeciles, unable to think for themselves; he spelled out every move and detail. To be fair, the man knew his business; and of course it was important to have a careful plan. The *signore* was very hard, very demanding, but he knew the ropes, that one; you had to give him credit.

Perugia shifted uncomfortably on the floor and continued to brood. For years he had struggled to become a skilled carpenter and a fine house painter, and what did he have to show for it? Loneliness, uncertainty, hard work, long months away from home; all for a handful of francs a day. But after tomorrow that would change; his fortune would be made. The *signore* had already given him cash and had promised him more francs than his tools and brushes could earn in twenty years. With luck, if it went well tomorrow, he could return to his beloved Lombardy; he would be the richest man in Dumenza, richer even than old Torelli with his olive and lemon orchards—and still young enough to enjoy it. Years ago, before leaving home, he had told his friend Tomaso, "I'm going away on foot; I'll come back in a car." And soon it would happen.

Yes, this scheme would set him free at last; it would also give him revenge on the French. Perugia detested the French, they were so petty and grasping. Why, half the paintings in this very museum had been stolen from Italy by that plunderer, Bonaparte. It had to be so—look at how many artists' names in the Louvre were Italian! *La Gioconda* herself was a good example; the French had no right to have her.

Living here in the middle of crowded Paris, Perugia had felt like an outcast, with no friends except for a small group of uprooted people like himself—carpenters, masons, painters, stonecutters, fine craftsmen who had left their poor towns in Italy and Sicily to find jobs in the cities of England and France. Yes, the French and the English were busy building great mansions and châteaus, but hard-working Italians were the ones who decorated them and made them beautiful. Not that their talents were appreciated. Even the Frenchmen whom Perugia worked with treated him with contempt. They had jeered at his accent, called him *"mangeur de macaroni,"* and when his head was turned away the *cretini* hid his tools and poured salt in his wine. But now he would get his own back; tomorrow the macaroni eater would show them a few surprises, thanks to the *signore*.

The *signore*—you could tell from the way he spoke that he wasn't French, still he was something of a mystery. Perugia and the others knew almost nothing about him, not even his real name; they knew only that the man was a perfectionist and very clever and had promised them great sums of money. Well, that was good enough. No doubt, the man had brains. He was in charge, and all they had to do now was to follow orders.

Shifting again on the hard unyielding floor, Perugia dozed fitfully and dreamed of Lombardy.

6

ON MONDAYS the Louvre came to life early, the ponderous gates swinging open at 6:30 A.M. to admit Georges Picquet's maintenance crews who would repair the week's ravages—plasterers, plumbers, electricians, carpenters, glaziers, as well as porters who could move anything, from fragile antiques to a thousand pounds of sculptured marble.

At about the same time, inside the Duchatel storeroom, Vincenzo Perugia got stiffly to his feet and massaged his sore limbs. He kicked his two helpers to awaken them, and put a stern finger to his lips. Listening for a moment at the concealed door, the carpenter could hear Picquet outside, giving orders in a stentorial voice. The maintenance boss would be everywhere today; they would have to move with care.

Silently, the three intruders opened the bundles they had brought and took out large white tunics made of a heavy linenlike material, which they pulled on over their jackets. These tunics, or blouses, were standard issue for workmen at the Louvre; the loose garments reaching almost to the knees served as uniform, passport and *carte d'identité* all rolled into one. At that time nothing else was needed: a worker wearing the official tunic on clean-up day was automatically legitimized and above suspicion.

When all was ready, Michele Lancelotti swung the strap of the big folding camera over his shoulder.

Perugia stared at him in surprise. *"Cosa fa?"* he hissed.

"My camera," Michele whispered. "I paid three hundred francs for it."

A fierce, muted argument ensued in which Michele was persuaded that a workman parading through the museum with an expensive camera on his shoulder was sure to attract attention. He conceded the matter at last— though reluctantly—and shoved the camera into a dusty corner behind a sculptor's stand. Perugia's straw hat, appropriate for a Sunday visitor but not for a museum worker, also presented a problem. The carpenter finally solved it by pulling up his tunic, jamming the hard brim into the waistband of his trousers, and dropping the garment over it; then, with a last look around and a nod to his companions, Perugia stepped to the door.

The men waited for several tense minutes, and at 7:05 slipped out into the empty Salle Duchatel. A long-handled broom stood against the wall; Vincent seized it and began sweeping energetically. Michele, after an unhappy look at the alcove containing his camera, drew a rag from his pocket and made a pretext of dusting railings and picture frames. Perugia strolled toward the adjoining Salon Carré, then drew back quickly; Georges Picquet was there in the next gallery with a crew of new workmen, standing right in front of the *Mona Lisa*. The custodian pointed to the Leonardo. "There," he announced with pride, "you see the most valuable painting in the Louvre. They say it's worth millions." The group circled the rest of the Carré, then moved into the connecting Picture Gallery, where maintenance work was under way.

Perugia, who had been watching from the arch, turned, signaled his partners, and hurried toward the da Vinci portrait, so familiar to him in its glass shadow box. Vincent Lancelotti joined him quickly, and Michele took up his post as lookout at the far door.

About three minutes later, the famous painting which the chief custodian had admired with such pride no longer graced the wall of the Salon Carré.

•   •

Contrary to general belief, the *Mona Lisa* isn't painted on canvas but on a solid panel of fine-grained white poplar wood, the favorite painting surface of Italian artists of the Renaissance. This panel, along with the large carved frame, the shadow box and the thick plate glass, added up to a fairly heavy load, and Valfierno had decided that two men were needed to manage it comfortably, with a third going along as scout and troubleshooter.

That particular morning, at least a dozen men were busy in the Picture Gallery. Several were replacing a broken windowpane, others were moving artwork so that plasterers could make repairs, a crew was washing down the floor, and some polished brass railings and fixtures. None of these took the slightest notice whatever of two white-bloused workers, trailed by a third, who quietly carried *La Joconde* out one end of the vast hall. On Mondays, pictures and art objects were always being shifted around the museum, all of it quite casually. Picquet or one of his assistants might call out, "Henri, this vase goes to the Rotonde," or "Pierre, the small Rembrandt to the photo studio, *vite*." It happened so regularly, in so offhand a way, that the thieves were able to function right under the unsuspecting eyes of the whole custodial staff.

Had Picquet himself seen them he might have intervened and started asking questions, but luckily for the trio he had hurried off to another part of the building. Given the general laxness, even Picquet might well have ignored their activities. Curators, restorers, photographers all were quite free to have artwork moved; and as Valfierno pointed out later, "No one ever questioned what a white-bloused workman did . . . If I wore a white blouse over my clothes, I could take down any picture, pick up any small piece of sculpture, grab a priceless Renaissance antique and carry it where I pleased, so long as I didn't attempt to leave the building."

The intruders were also helped by the museum's lopsided security plan. In those years the Louvre's directors worried far more about vandalism than about theft. The notion that someone might actually try to steal a great masterpiece was unthinkable, it simply wasn't done. On the other hand, Parisians took their art seriously; the lunatic fringe was a reality, and valuable work was always prey to attack with knives, nailfiles, scissors, hammers, sharp umbrella tips and containers of acid. As a result there were well over one hundred men on security duty *during routine visiting hours,* many of them plainclothes detectives watching for potential troublemakers. But on clean-up days with the public barred, this force was trimmed to a tiny fraction of the normal complement, which vastly improved the odds for Perugia and the Lancelottis.

Now, having deftly unhooked *La Joconde* from the wall of the Carré, the thieves convoyed her unchallenged through the Grande Galerie, across a corner of the Salle des Sept Mètres, where other men were working, then through a door opening on a narrow, dimly lit service stairway.

Perugia had supplied himself with an assortment of small tools. Safe behind the service door, he took a knife and sliced away the heavy tapes which held the panel in its frame. The frame, the box and the glass cover were pushed into a dark corner of the landing; then, carrying the precious panel, Perugia bounded downstairs with the brothers at his heels.

At the bottom of the stairs, calamity awaited. For security reasons, all service doors leading from the museum's ground floor were kept locked. The *signore* had supplied Perugia with a duplicate key made from a wax impression, which would open this particular door and give them access to a courtyard, but the wax impression wasn't too reliable, and Valfierno had repeatedly warned Perugia to test the key ahead of time. The carpenter had neglected to do so, and now, as he inserted it and tried to open the door, nothing happened. Panicking, he tried again and again, twisting and jiggling the key, but the door wouldn't budge. While the Lancelottis hovered over him anxiously, Perugia struggled with the lock. Every second's delay obviously meant danger; retracing their steps would be risky, and now that the painting was out of its frame they were completely vulnerable.

For a few moments it appeared that the *signore*'s noble plan would self-destruct in a cramped, musty stairwell. But Perugia had other ideas. Sending Michele back upstairs to keep watch, he pulled out a screwdriver and started to dismantle the stubborn lock. The carpenter, working rapidly, removed the bronze doorknob, dropped it into a pocket of his jacket and began to unscrew the face plate. He had this halfway off when Michele's frightened face appeared over the railing.

"*Attenti!* Somebody's coming!"

Perugia and Vincent froze at the balky door and stared at each other in alarm.

Moments later the Louvre's official plumber, a spare gangling man named Sauvet, came trudging down the stairs carrying his tool kit. He noticed two unhappy-looking workmen standing in the dim light below him, but saw nothing of the *Mona Lisa,* which Perugia had slipped up under his tunic and was holding in place with an elbow while keeping that side turned away.

Now Perugia showed the presence of mind which the Marqués had been depending on. Glaring at the plumber, he took the offensive.

"Some idiot stole the doorknob," he shouted, "*Che follia,* what are we supposed to do? How do we get out of here, crawl through the keyhole?"

"Calm. Stay calm," Sauvet said soothingly. Using a key of his own, he turned the lock, reached in with his pliers, twisted the latch bar, and opened the door.

With the brothers behind him and his elbow still held rigidly, Perugia stalked out, looking very put upon.

Sauvet, hurrying off to his chores, turned back with a final word. "I'll make out a slip," he said, "but you'd better leave that door open so it won't bother anyone else."

The three men now found themselves in a small inner courtyard known as the Cour du Sphinx. From there, according to plan, they crossed an adjoining gallery, the Salle d'Afrique, and entered a larger quadrangle, the Cour Visconti. On the south wall of this court was a vestibule with a heavy door which stood wide open to the street, and Perugia, with *La Joconde* under his tunic, was a scant forty feet from freedom. But to the trespassers' dismay, a uniformed guard (one of the few on duty that morning) was mopping the vestibule and effectively blocking their path.

After vacillating briefly, the thieves took cover behind some large packing crates. Michele and Vincent darted agonized glances at Perugia, but the stubborn carpenter refused to be discouraged; they were much too close to give up. He peered anxiously around the yard, trying to remember the various diagrams the *signore* had shown him. There was another door opposite, but Perugia could see that it was heavily padlocked. Retracing their steps now would be even riskier than before. So they had no other choice: the only logical route was out through the Visconti Gate—and with the guard standing there, it was impossible. The house painter's eyes darted about as he fought a mounting panic. Many windows opened onto the courtyard; at any moment somebody might look out, see three workmen behaving suspiciously, and come down to investigate. They had to break out of the trap, and quickly.

Once again an incredible blend of luck and timing came to the gang's rescue. That morning the regular porter had failed to show up, and the duty guard was filling in for him by swabbing the entranceway. Now he decided that he needed clean water, and since there was nobody on hand to run errands he picked up the pail and sauntered off to the utility room, leaving the vestibule unattended. Watching from their hiding place, the men quickly removed their white blouses. Perugia wrapped his tunic around the stolen panel and clapped on his straw hat. Then, a few minutes short of 8 A.M., while the rest of the city was rousing itself for the day, the marauders stepped out into the soft Paris sunshine.

The men turned right on the Quai du Louvre, walking briskly. As they hurried along, Perugia felt something odd thumping in his jacket pocket. Reaching in, he found the heavy doorknob which he had removed earlier, and without giving it a thought he tossed the knob over a fence into a nearby ditch. A passing laborer happened to witness this, and while it meant nothing to him at that moment, it would prove important later.

Around the corner of the museum on the Rue des Tuileries (now the Avenue Général-Lemonnier) a taxi was waiting, the driver bribed to collect three passengers, deliver them to a certain street corner near Les Halles, and keep his mouth shut afterward. The men climbed in quickly and, as the cab rattled along the Rue St.-Honoré, exchanged broad grins and thumped one another delightedly on the back. Perugia sat in triumph with the rectangular white package on his lap, feeling like a monarch. *Molto facile*—all so simple and easy, like sipping a smooth wine. The carpenter looked at his watch; it had taken them, from the time they left their hiding place, about one hour to steal the *Mona Lisa*.

It would be, surprisingly, another twenty-seven hours before anyone in the Louvre realized that the portrait was missing.

PART TWO

The Ruse

In art there is strenuous competition; the rare becomes desirable precisely because no one else can have it. To the forger, this situation is irresistible.

—LAWRENCE JEPPSON,
The Fabulous Frauds

7

AFTER THEY HAD MADE OFF with the painting the gang's first rendezvous was apparently the garret room of one Françoise Séguenot, on a dingy street near Les Halles called the Rue St.-Merri. Today this street, in the shadow of Paris's spectacular attraction, the Pompidou Center of Art and Culture, sparkles with chic cafés and trendy boutiques; but in 1911 it was a seedy working-class area on the fringe of the Halles Centrales, the great sprawling marketplace with its thousands of stalls and offices which supplied food to half of France.

Mme. Séguenot, fortyish, married several times before and at that point the mistress of Vincent Lancelotti, was a *blanchisseuse*, one of the city's vast army of washerwomen, and her shabby anonymous room was well suited to Valfierno's purposes. According to plan, Perugia left the painting there with his friends; then to cover himself he hurried to his current job, which was with a painting contractor named Perrotti on the Rue de Maubeuge. Normally expected to be at work at seven, Perugia arrived shortly after nine, explaining that he had overslept and wasn't feeling well. The excuse was accepted without question; in fact, it helped explain his uncommon pallor and nervousness during the day.

Finished with work at last, Perugia hastened back to the Rue St.-Merri; and shortly after, returning from Longchamp, the Marqués appeared at the rendezvous and satisfied himself that the trio had indeed pulled off the coup of the century. It was a moment which had long been awaited, and Valfierno savored it fully. He examined the *Mona Lisa* with delight—she was smiling at him as though sharing the preposterous joke—and listened intently as the carpenter described the morning's events. Drawing out a copious billfold, Valfierno paid them all handsomely (including the wide-eyed Mme. Séguenot) and swore the group to silence; if they continued to follow orders, the *signore* added, more cash would soon be forthcoming. He and Perugia then went out together for a long walk and some serious conversation.

Since he had once worked at the Louvre, it was possible, the *signore* pointed out, that Perugia would receive a visit from the police. There was no cause for alarm; it would doubtless be a routine check, and Perugia could be quite open and "cooperative." After—and only after—the investigators had given him a clean bill of health was he to reclaim the panel from Madame Séguenot and take it back to his own room on the Rue de l'Hôpital-St.-Louis, in the Tenth Arrondissement. After Perugia retrieved the portrait, Valfierno went on, he was to burn the tunic, wrap the panel in a large protective cloth and hide it away safely, perhaps behind a false wall in his closet.

"I will be traveling for a while," the *signore* explained, "but you'll hear from me periodically. Guard *La Joconde* with care and wait for instructions; in the meantime go about your own affairs in a quiet, normal way."

Once again the Marqués reminded the anxious Perugia of his previous scrapes with the law and described in blunt terms what would happen to him if there were any further slipups. Near the Place des Vosges—the lovely old square built for King Henri IV, coincidentally one of the earliest patrons of the Louvre—the conspirators parted company.

On his way back to his hotel the Marqués stopped at

a cable office and sent several radio messages to addresses
in New York City; and at the concierge's desk he booked
passage for himself on a steamship bound for the United
States. Then, collecting an armload of afternoon newspapers, he went to his suite and leafed through them.

The headlines were predictable. The Germans were
rattling their sabers again, this time over France's new
protectorate in Morocco; the Kaiser, fuming, had ordered
a gunboat to Agadir to "protect German interests," and
now there was a real threat of war in North Africa. Closer
at home, France's first amphibious aircraft, the Voisin
Canard, was successfully test-flown and landed safely on the
Seine River at Billancourt. Tobacco prices had dropped;
the popular new Hungarian cigarettes called Gauloises
were selling for only seventy centimes a pack. Diaghilev's
Ballets Russes had taken all Paris by storm, the critics
raving particularly about Igor Stravinsky's brilliant
Petrouchka ballet and Nijinsky's dancing in *Spectre de la
Rose.* The National Railway Workers were meeting in
Belleville to plan their strike strategy, although according
to one observer "more insults than ideas were exchanged."
And Paris's columnists were still gossiping over the mysterious death of the chanteuse Geneviève Lantelme, fifth
wife of the wealthy Alfred Edwards. The glamorous singer
had drowned in the Rhine River when she fell or jumped
from the Edwards' yacht, *L'Aimée,* and there were rumors
that drugs and alcohol were involved. Lantelme had been
buried at Père Lachaise, the press gravely reported, "just
as she was taken out of the Rhine, still wearing her jewels
and the superb three-strand pearl necklace."

Valfierno tossed the papers aside in annoyance. There
was no mention anywhere, in any of them, of the disappearance of France's most treasured masterpiece.

He leaned back in his armchair and stared thought-
fully at the ceiling. Of course there could be only two

explanations. Either the theft hadn't been discovered—incredible but not impossible—or the Louvre's officials were deliberately hushing it up. Perhaps he had underestimated them; could Perugia have left some clues which they were now quietly tracking down? Was the whole venture, teetering on the edge of success, about to disintegrate?

Well, it was surely too early to tell; he'd have to be patient a while longer. But the last thing he wanted now was secrecy; for this ruse to work, a bombshell would have to drop. And loudly. It was essential for a startled world to read that the priceless Leonardo had been plucked from the Louvre in broad daylight, and that no one had the slightest idea where it could be found.

8

VINCENZO PERUGIA relaxed on the creaky bed and strummed a few chords on his mandolin. Music helped him to think.

The *signore* was a puzzle—why had he left the painting with Séguenot instead of carrying it away? Perugia thought surely the man would rush off with it and arrange a secret sale to one of his millionaires. Well, he was careful, that one; doubtless he knew what he was doing. Everything had gone so smoothly, just as the man had planned—almost a miracle—and now they had only to be patient. But that *vacca*, Lancelotti's woman—how could the *signore* trust her? She was stupid. Unreliable. He himself would be glad when this waiting was over and he could hide the *Gioconda* in his own place, where it would be safe.

Perugia played a few bars of "Mattinata," his favorite, and thought about his good luck. Soon he would drive right down the main street of Dumenza in a big Daimler, or a Lozier roadster with a folding top, or maybe one of those fine models made by his countryman Ettore Bugatti. A new car with a brass horn next to the driver's seat. He thought of his parents, his sister, his three brothers—how their eyes would pop!

The carpenter put his mandolin aside, along with his daydreams. It was important now to be practical. When the French discovered that their precious painting was gone there would be a great alarm; police would be everywhere, and since he had worked at the Louvre he might be a suspect. The *signore* had warned him to be very careful, very alert. Lips sealed. Eyes and ears open. It would be difficult to force himself to behave in a normal way and go to work every day as though nothing had changed.

Yes, that would be the hardest for him—to pretend all was the same when he knew that all was different. But the French were fools; they didn't frighten Vincenzo Perugia. He would play his part like an actor. He could be very cunning if necessary, and now there was a fortune at stake. The *capo* had been generous with him, and would be even more so. He was strange, that one; not easy to understand. But a man of vision and ideas, worth trusting. So he himself would try to stay calm and do his duty, and let the *signore* do the rest.

9

VALFIERNO'S PROJECT had had its origins in the Salon Carré, under the collusive gaze of the lady herself.

On a cold gray afternoon toward the end of 1910, he and Chaudron had gone to the museum to inspect the new glass coverings. By that time all the protective cases were in place, though the wave of complaints hadn't subsided. Indignant letters still cropped up in the press, and angry editorials in the art publications; and as an act of protest one young novelist had brought his shaving equipment to the Salon Carré and proceeded to shave himself, using his reflection in the glass on the *Mona Lisa*. Despite the furor, Homolle stood firm; the shadow boxes were there to stay, since they served to frustrate vandals.

They also served to draw Eduardo de Valfierno to the Louvre, and that afternoon as he and Chaudron studied the portrait the notion began to flower.

"Could you," the Marqués casually asked Chaudron, "make an exact copy of this?"

Narrowing his eyes, the master forger leaned over for a closer look at the *Mona Lisa*. "One has the problem," he mused, "of da Vinci's *sfumatura*; the soft outlines, the smoothly blended tones. Very subtle, very difficult to capture. But it can be done, yes."

"Could you perhaps make *more* than one copy?"

Chaudron regarded him curiously. "I would say yes, given enough time, but I don't understand—"

Valfierno took the artist's thin arm and guided him toward the marble staircase. "Let us explore the matter elsewhere."

Seated at the Vachette in a corner well out of general earshot, the Marqués evolved his plan. In the old days in Buenos Aires, he later told his American Boswell, he had occasionally sold a Murillo or a Francisco de Zurbarán "from the wall." This meant, in his parlance, that a painting actually hanging in a museum was sold to a venal buyer with the tacit understanding that it might soon "become available." The euphemism covered a ruse as simple as it was foolproof; and all it required was to bribe a few cooperative museum guards to look the other way and guarantee a few minutes of privacy.

The intended mark (somebody who lived far from Buenos Aires and wasn't likely to pay a return visit) was invited to the museum and shown the painting in question. By this time he had already signaled his interest, in fact eagerness, to acquire so magnificent an Old Master. With the room cleared (by arrangement) of other visitors, the Marqués would step up to the picture and pull one edge of the frame a few inches away from the wall. The client was then invited to take his pen and make a secret mark on the back of the canvas—a signature, symbol, hieroglyph, anything that he could later identify. It was, Eduardo would point out tactfully, handy insurance for the purchaser. His victims were always happy to comply; and as Lawrence Jeppson, who described Valfierno's scheme, has noted, "some signatures were as flourishing and as unfakable as a bank officer's name on a cashier's check, others ingenious ciphers hidden in a corner." One suspicious cattle baron went even further: taking a penknife from his pocket, he hacked a jagged bit of canvas from the edge where it was folded back over the wooden stretchers. The Texan pocketed the canvas fragment, announcing that he would match it against the edge of the canvas when it was eventually delivered, and the Marqués complimented him on his shrewdness.

In due time this "stolen" masterpiece was shipped north of the Rio Grande, where the pleased client found that his jagged edge of canvas matched perfectly. What he and the other victims didn't know was that, days earlier, an excellent forgery by Yves Chaudron had been fitted into place behind the original, with both painted surfaces facing the same way. The forged copy was measured with care so that the fit was snug, the double stretchers were covered with tape, and in the poorly lighted museum the deception easily escaped notice. So when a victim carefully code-marked a painting he was, Valfierno noted, "really marking the back of the copy, and that's what he got." It was, in effect, an aesthetic variation of the age-old gypsy switch—and, given the right blend of greed and naïveté, it worked.

Before each fraud was delivered it was taken back to Chaudron's studio, removed from its stretcher frame and hidden inside a cheap rolled-up rug. This lent an air of veracity to the transaction and helped cover the fact that the dimensions of the copy and the original were slightly different. The Marqués also made a point afterward of forwarding to his victims a few "newspaper clippings" from South American papers—counterfeited by a local printer—reporting that a certain Murillo or Zurbarán had been brazenly carried off by unknown desperadoes. If by any chance one of Valfierno's dupes returned to the city and saw the picture still on the museum wall, he would simply be told that it was a copy, obtained by the embarrassed directors to replace the stolen original. "Their painting," the Marqués would reassure his client (he was an expert reassurer), "is a substitute, a clever forgery. *You,* dear sir, own the real one."

Valfierno the master swindler knew that to be successful every confidence game needed two equally larcenous parties—not only a dishonest victimizer but a dishonest victim; he knew also that a dupe could be naïve, but was never innocent.

Now, sitting over their wine, he suggested to Chaudron that they might use a variation of the old plan to sell *La Joconde,* not once but several times. "I think," he said, "we could dispose of as many as you can produce."

Chaudron stared at him in disbelief. It was one thing to fool a simpleton over an obscure Murillo hanging in a small museum in Buenos Aires; but the great *Mona Lisa?* That was *formidable*—something altogether different. The idea struck him as not just foolhardy but impossible.

"There are certain wealthy people, as you know," the Marqués went on serenely, "who will buy anything, illegal or not, if they think it rare enough. I'm still in contact with a number of them."

The forger shook his head nervously. "Marqués, what are you saying? Paris isn't Buenos Aires. The Leonardo is a great masterpiece, the most famous in the world. Thousands of people go to the museum every day just to look at it; they can see the *Mona Lisa* there on the wall, right in front of their eyes. The portrait is too well known; if we pretended to steal it, who in his right mind would believe us?"

Valfierno nodded. "Quite so, and that's precisely why this time we won't pretend. No more make-believe thefts, my dear Chaudron; no more fake news clippings for a fool gringo who can't read Spanish to begin with. No, this time we will find somebody skilled enough to remove *La Joconde* from the museum for us."

Chaudron, his eyes growing wide in his gaunt face, stared in fascination at the debonair gray-haired man.

"Real headlines this time," the Marqués continued. "Real stories in newspapers all over the world. To convince our nervous buyers. But first—" he leaned over with a smile and tapped the artist's bony knee—"first we must have our masterpieces."

10

THAT WINTER Yves Chaudron began to clone the *Mona Lisa,* and in doing so he carried on a tradition as old as art itself.

In the course of history just about everything of value has at some time been forged or counterfeited. The list

includes not only artwork but furniture, old maps, book-
bindings, musical instruments, weapons, paperweights,
rare stamps, snuffboxes, stock certificates, historic letters
and documents, coins and paper money, costumes and
carpets, porcelain, silver candlesticks, autographs, costly
watches, antique jewelry—whatever can bring a fat price
in a seller's market.

An Egyptian papyrus three thousand years old, now
in the Stockholm Museum, gives instructions on how to
forge gemstones from colored glass; and according to
Seneca there were Roman workshops in Caesar's time devoted to counterfeiting precious jewels and pearls. Falsify-
ing things of value is a by-product of the law of supply and
demand. Critic Frank Jewett Mather wrote years ago,
"Whenever there is a scarcity of any sort of object in the
art market, and corresponding dearness, there will be
forgeries." Or as one art dealer has put it, "Anything that
gets expensive gets faked."

In the period when nations built empires it was said
that "trade follows the flag," and in a similar way art
forgery follows the tastes of society. Fad and fashion have
always played their part: as certain items become rare they
obviously grow in value, and at that point the fakers move
in. So at the height of the Roman Empire, when the art of
ancient Greece was eagerly collected, sculptors busily
forged Hellenic pieces. In a thirteenth-century turnabout,
Venetian mosaic workers imitated the art of early Rome.
Skilled European craftsmen in the 1500s turned out car-
loads of sham Oriental porcelain—*porcellana contrefatta*—
which found ready buyers. During the eighteenth and nineteenth centuries antiques markets were flooded with imita-
tion Meissen ware. In more recent times there has been a
thriving traffic in fake pre-Columbian art and African
primitive carvings; and through all these years, museum
curators and private collectors have been had again and
again by sellers of fraudulent sculpture and paintings.

In his youth even the great Michelangelo Buonarroti tried a bit of flimflam. Early in his career the sculptor was a student of Ghirlandajo and a protégé of Lorenzo de' Medici, who had an eye for latent genius. Lorenzo commissioned the young artist to create some pieces for his private park, and Michelangelo did so successfully. The Florentine nobleman was delighted with these new carvings, except for one small figure called the *Sleeping Cupid*. It was beautiful, Lorenzo agreed, though not quite suitable for his magnificent gardens. But he had an interesting idea. The little sculpture could be artificially aged and predated some fifteen hundred years, so that "it could be sold in Rome as an antique." Michelangelo, dazzled at the prospect of an inflated fee—and hardly in a position to oppose his powerful patron—agreed to the deception.

On Lorenzo's advice the *Sleeping Cupid* was buried for a while in sour earth—soil with a high acid content—which would convincingly darken and pit the stone. It was then sent to a prominent art dealer in Rome named Baldassare del Milanese. The dealer, pleased with this "archaic" sculpture and apparently in on the scheme, sold it to Cardinal Riario of San Giorgio for two hundred gold ducats, Michelangelo's share being a skimpy fifteen percent.

But it wasn't long before rumors got back to the cardinal, who sent an emissary to investigate. Lorenzo, suddenly fearful of being implicated, denied any part in the hoax, but the young sculptor admitted everything, and rather proudly. At which point an indignant Cardinal Riario returned the sculpture to Baldassare and demanded his ducats back. So in the rich lore of art forgery a special place belongs to the cardinal who wouldn't be hoodwinked —and got a refund on a genuine Michelangelo.

The little sculpture featured in the Episode of the Duped Cardinal was eventually lost, but a later version of the *Sleeping Cupid,* believed to be a seventeenth-century copy, is now at the Museo di Antichità in Turin.

Michelangelo's fling at Florentine larceny wasn't typical, since in his case the "fake" outdid the work being simulated. But most forgeries at their best are pallid imitations of the originals, and the skills of a copyist— even a brilliant one like Chaudron—can't equal the gifts of the geniuses being plagiarized.

Most art forgers are failed sculptors or painters. Like all humans they aren't easy to pigeonhole, but they seem to share a number of traits. "The potential forger of works of art," according to Professor Mather, "is first of all a passionate antiquarian; next he is a craftsman; and finally he is poor." Europe's expert on art fraud, Frank Arnau, has written that "the majority of forgers, and by no means the least gifted, practice their craft or trade—however one cares to describe it—for purely materialistic reasons. A perfectly forged Corot is easier to sell than a good genuine work by an unknown." And, he might have added, it brings a much fancier price.

The typical forger is by and large impatient, immature, versatile, affable, frustrated, daring, luxury-loving and hungry for artistic success—the kind of success denied to his own personal creations. The shadowy Yves Chaudron displayed some of these traits, but he had one advantage over others in his craft: he was without vanity. Case records of forgeries indicate that many swindlers sooner or later overstep themselves and grow careless, because the more successful the hoax the greater the urge for recognition. In time a forger begins to feel invincible, talks too much, gets slipshod in his work and brings on inevitable disaster.

Chaudron was spared all that. Quiet, self-effacing, a dedicated technician and master of other painters' styles, he was able to stay detached, to submerge himself totally in his "product." Instead of soothing his ego Chaudron became a mirror, reflecting back no more and no less than what was given; and now, under the Marqués de Valfierno's guidance, established in a tiny studio in Montmartre, he began his most difficult assignment.

The conjurer's first job was to visit the Louvre and make an exact copy of the *Mona Lisa* so as to capture the portrait's subtle colors and tonal variations. In keeping with museum rules, Chaudron's copy was smaller than the original—about three-quarters actual size. He worked quickly and completed his version in a matter of days, during which period he kept a low profile and evidently wasn't noticed by any of the guards or visitors. Copyists at that time were, of course, a normal part of the museum's landscape; the *Mona Lisa* was a popular subject; students, amateurs and professional artists came often to the Salon Carré to paint and sketch the famed Lisa del Giocondo. So Chaudron sat and worked quietly, all but invisible, while hundreds of people flowed around him oblivious to the crime just beginning to unfold. Since he wanted to attract as little attention as possible, it is unlikely that the forger left any of his supplies overnight in the Duchatel storeroom, the alcove which would play its own part in the coming scenario.

When his small copy was finished, the next task was to find suitably aged wooden panels. At some point in its murky history the sides of this portrait had apparently been cropped, and the dimensions of the Louvre panel were now roughly thirty and a half inches high and twenty-one inches wide. Poking around in Paris's antique shops, Chaudron found a number of old panel paintings of mediocre quality; he bought these, trimmed them as needed, and scraped off the original pigment. At considerable cost, Valfierno also came up with an antique Italian cupboard the backboard of which was cut into rectangles of the right size. The artist now had authentic surfaces on which to create his visual sophistry.

Chaudron had spent much time with a magnifying glass studying the original portrait, and he planned, if he could, to duplicate Leonardo's palette and brush strokes. To transfer his scale version of *La Joconde* to the old panels, he used a balopticon, a device which projects enlarged images by reflected light. Several good photographs of the painting also supplied measurements and details. The project was helped by the fact that a great deal is actually known about the painting methods of the Old Masters. In the libraries of Paris, records were available ranging from the eighth-century Lucca Manuscript, which deals with the manufacture of vegetable pigments and staining oils, to the *Mappae claviculae,* a Venetian treatise of the thirteenth century, and the *Hermeneia* of Dionysus, a classic handbook on the rules of Byzantine painting. Most useful of all to Chaudron was Cennino Cennini's *Trattato della pittura,* a craftsman's text which first appeared in 1390 and was used for decades by all serious painters, including Leonardo da Vinci.

In Renaissance times, preparing the gesso, or ground for an oil painting was a complicated process. According to the *Trattato*—and doubtlessly followed by Leonardo—it involved primer coats of gum mastic, turpentine and white lead, followed by several layers of alcohol and arsenic. Next came a coating of linseed oil rubbed in slowly with the heel of the hand; the panel was then washed with urine to remove any remaining grease, and finally the surface was buffed and honed repeatedly until a hard, bone-white finish was created.

Now the surface was ready for actual painting, which involved another set of procedures. Masters such as Leonardo, Raphael, Titian and Van Eyck used to apply layer after layer of pigment and thin color glazes interspersed with coats of varnish, which helped to create a sense of luminous dimension instead of the flat "cutout" look of earlier periods. The artist-technicians of the Renaissance literally built up their scenes with scores of these color washes, applied slowly and painstakingly, day after day. Naturally, Chaudron couldn't match so laborious a process. "Not even the most conscientious forger," Frank Arnau points out, "can copy the extraordinarily complicated techniques of the great masters." Shortcuts were needed, and the former art restorer used them skillfully. By matching colors with care and applying them efficiently he was able to create a *surface* effect highly convincing to untrained eyes.

Chaudron avoided the classic error made by less experienced deceivers: he used only those pigments known to have been used by Leonardo, shunning colors such as cobalt blue, cadmium yellow and zinc white which didn't appear in painters' ateliers until years later. Many a hardworking forger has been tripped up by trivial details—fastening the hinges of a medieval diptych, for example, with machine-made instead of hand-made nails, or using modern acids (detectable by chemical means) to "age" an otherwise flawless marble sculpture. Chaudron not only avoided such pitfalls but brought to his cloned madonnas a high degree of sensitivity, style and expressiveness.

As each portrait was completed, the artist's next problem was to duplicate the fine hairline cracks, known as *craquelure,* which the passing of time inflicts on almost all old painted surfaces. On canvas-based pictures, *craquelure* usually forms graceful random patterns; on panel paintings it tends to follow the grain of the wood.

A close look at the Louvre's *Mona Lisa*—or at an enlarged reproduction—shows it to be covered with a subtle network of these delicate cracks, particularly noticeable on the face, chest and hands. Interestingly enough, *craquelure* doesn't interfere with the aesthetic quality of an Old Master, yet its presence is obvious, and it adds a necessary degree of age and authenticity. To telescope four hundred years of time quickly, Chaudron applied two coats of clear varnish to his finished portraits. The bottom coat, or underlayer, was a slow-drying varnish; the top layer was faster-drying. He then placed each panel under a large spinning fan. The blasts of cold air plus the action of the two varnish coats, drying at sharply different rates, soon caused a splendid web of *craquelure* to appear. Later, after the varnish had completely dried, the forger gently rubbed dust into the cracks with a pad of cotton wool.

To heighten the impression of aging, Chaudron added spots of powdered graphite as "soot marks"; he also stained the backs of the panels with oil and tannic acid.

Though accurate and convincing, these master forgeries were not meant, of course, to be examined by experts or art connoisseurs; the panels were intended rather for the untrained eyes of a few collectors whose pocketbooks matched their avarice, and who were far more interested in acquisition than in close examination.

Today there are many technical procedures for evaluating paintings and detecting frauds, among them microphotography, carbon dating, chemical analysis, color spectroscopy, infrared and ultraviolet scanning, gamma-ray measurements, and a brand-new technique using neutron beams, called autoradiography. At the turn of the century, however, the only new technological development was X-ray photography—and in fact, in 1900, the *Mona Lisa* became one of the first Louvre masterpieces to be so X-rayed. But Valfierno's prospects had no access to this technique nor any interest in it whatever. At that time authenticating a picture—determining its true pedigree or provenance—depended chiefly on reliable historical or personal records and, most important of all, sensitive evaluation by experts.

The victims of the ruse were neither expert nor particularly sensitive; their only aim was to acquire something which *nobody else had,* and for that purpose Chaudron's excellent fakes were more than adequate.

In all, Valfierno had his forger create six facsimiles, five of which were destined for sale in North America and the sixth for a buyer in Brazil. To attempt more than that, he felt, would require too much time and might possibly endanger the whole plan.

As it was, the project took all of Chaudron's effort and concentration. Over a period of months the obsessive painter worked on his panels every day and in the evenings slipped out to wander the narrow streets of Montmartre. And when his copies were completed, the next phase of the scheme was put in motion.

11

PIER 59 in New York City, where the *Mauretania* was disembarking its passengers, was a scene of vast ordered chaos as hundreds of travelers moved through the rituals of arrival.

The customs officer nodded to a well-dressed courtly gentleman in front of him and glanced at the name and the picture on his passport. A marqués, no less, and well off, judging from the elegant steamer trunk and matched suitcases of heavy leather. The man also had a trim, brass-fitted case with him which contained some oil paintings— several fine copies of a Flemish landscape, a facsimile of a still life by Chardin, and a copy of the *Mona Lisa* painted on wood. The Marqués declared all these to be what they were, good replicas, and mentioned that he was bringing them as gifts for friends. He also produced bills of sale for the items from an established Paris dealer.

To the customs official it was a routine matter. In those years before the development of fine art books and color reproductions, people of means often bought hand-made copies of old paintings. What better way to adorn the walls of their lavish homes or impress their friends with their taste and culture? Americans abroad liked to pick up costly souvenirs; as a result, facsimile Rembrandts, Rubens, Vermeers, Corots, Raphaels and other masters flowed across the Atlantic. The *Mona Lisa* became in a sense a seasoned traveler, and duplicate versions of the portrait aroused no suspicion. After all, as everyone knew and could see, the real da Vinci was in its proper place on a wall of the Louvre; Lisa del Giocondo was safe at home. So in due course the Marqués and his pictures were waved past the barriers.

One week later two more copies of the *Mona Lisa* arrived on the liner *Olympic* in the care of a tall, aristocratic Englishman. These were also cleared quickly. Three other portraits, sent by overseas cargo, were collected by the Marqués at the offices of the Port of New York, and one panel was then rerouted to Brazil.

By June of 1911, all six of Chaudron's forgeries had been safely brought out of France, five to be stored in a Manhattan warehouse and the sixth tucked away in a bank vault in Rio de Janeiro.

Some months before, another delicate phase had begun; and for this two experts worked closely with Valfierno. One was a distinguished-looking British ex-diplomat with international connections, the other an American "investment counselor" who had entree into social and moneyed circles in the United States. For reasons of his own, Valfierno never disclosed the identities of these two men; nonetheless one can hazard a guess.

In 1914, U.S. postal inspectors raided the New York offices of one James W. Ryan, a suave trickster whose forte was the peddling of phony investments. Since some of this work involved mail fraud, he became known to the authorities as "the Postal Kid," an alias which Ryan always felt lacked proper dignity. During that raid the officials found an extensive, neatly kept file catalogue of "prospects"; the affable Ryan obviously knew everyone, and his tidy records comprised a who's who of New York's elite with emphasis on wealthy art fanciers. The police withheld the prominent names listed on these cards, but some of Ryan's entries became known; for example: "Prides himself on his knowledge of art . . . will buy any picture if flattered into believing he knows all about it." Other cards and entries dealt with the prospects' tastes in paintings, their likes, dislikes, personal approachability and so on. Jim Ryan, genial and cultivated, moved with ease through art society and would have fit perfectly into Valfierno's plans. Was he perhaps the "American connection"? Certainly his mini-dossiers contained information which the Marqués greatly valued and may indeed have used.

Then in August 1933, sometime after Valfierno's death, an English con man named Jack Dean, well known to Scotland Yard, startled London by implicating himself in the earlier theft of the *Mona Lisa*. Dean wasn't of the proper social caliber, but his bizarre story (to be detailed later) paralleled the known facts of Valfierno's ruse. Dean's references to the crime, and his close knowledge of its covert details, gives rise to a possible connection with the Marqués's British confederate.

Whether Ryan and Dean did play some role in all this or were merely coincidental figures may never fully be determined; in any event, while Chaudron was busy in Paris, Valfierno's little cabal began its careful sales campaign in North and South America. Certain prospects were contacted one by one: buyers who might be interested in owning the most famous portrait in the world, provided— borrowing a euphemism from the old Buenos Aires days— it were to mysteriously "become available."

This sales goal wasn't as improbable as it might sound. "The gift of the confidence man," Lawrence Jeppson wrote, "lies in being able to spot people susceptible to corruption." Aware of this, the trio picked their targets with care, avoiding knowledgeable and sophisticated collectors such as Andrew Carnegie, John Pierpont Morgan and Henry Clay Frick, and concentrating on the *arrivistes,* who were often as unscrupulous in acquiring art as they had been in building their fortunes. At one point Valfierno referred to these rugged individualists as "horny-handed and well-heeled men lacking in any background of culture, or knowledge of art," and confided that dealing with them was simply a matter of striking the right tone and "preparing them mentally."

Experienced pirates like Valfierno were not only energetic manipulators but instinctive psychologists. John Maxtone-Graham, writing of that special breed of gamblers and card sharps who plied the great ocean liners during the early 1900s, understood the ambience they tried to create for their victims:

> Imagine the hours of jovial play, interspersed with good whiskey and conversation. The careful façade of good will, companionship and flattery, set against the civilized pace of shipboard life, made the whole proposition seem quite legitimate. The skill of the gambler lay more in this critical establishment of mood than in the manipulation of cards.

The Marqués and his associates knew people and how to maneuver them. When they courted a prospect, everything they said or did had a dual purpose: to lull a client's possible suspicions and at the same time whet his dishonest appetites. Their marks were self-made men of limited education and great wealth—timber tycoons, heads of small banks, railroad executives, wheat merchants, cattle kings; and in Brazil there were owners of rubber plantations in the Amazon basin, who had built palaces for themselves in the booming city of Manaus. Some of these millionaires, perhaps in an effort to buy the cultivated backgrounds they were originally denied, became passionate collectors of fine art.

The psychologist Dr. Henry Codet, who made a study of art addicts, found that they have four basic traits in common: a strong possessive instinct, a need for spontaneous activity, a drive to surpass themselves and lastly a great desire for social standing. In some cases the passion for collecting becomes a neurotic obsession, a mania that resembles the fever of compulsive gambling.

Pierre Cabanne, historian of the great collections, notes that this urge can sometimes destroy all sense of moral values, and that compulsive acquirers may even "become thieves and crooks, robbing other people of their capital, or embezzling public funds, and running on bankruptcies that ruin themselves and those who have been unlucky enough to trust them." He cites the example of a Barcelona dealer in antique books, one Don Vincente, who went so far as to murder the owner of a rare volume he coveted. The dealer (his case is documented in Spanish police files) hoped to acquire his prize by purchasing it from the dead man's estate. As Cabanne points out, the possessive drive is akin to love of battle, and an avid collector has a strong urge "to conquer the object he wants to own; hostility, rivalry and sharp practice only whet his appetite and rouse his fighting instincts. He stops short of no means, no ruse, trick or maneuver to get what he wants, and he no sooner has it than he forgets all the trials it has cost him as he sets out in pursuit of his next prize."

Assuredly this analysis doesn't apply to dedicated

connoisseurs such as the Carnegies, the Rockefellers and the Wideners, or devotees like J. P. Morgan, Philip Lehman, Samuel Kress, Gertrude Vanderbilt Whitney, Albert Barnes, Andrew Mellon, Isabella Stewart Gardner. Those collectors, though fiercely competitive, never lost a sense of proportion, and not only promoted art but with their patronage kept many a struggling painter, gallery and museum solvent.

As they acquired their valuable drawings, paintings and sculpture, some of these collectors were victimized by swindlers and wound up with numerous fakes and forgeries. In the case of Morgan, as will be seen, he was also implicated by rumor and innuendo in the theft of the *Mona Lisa* and had to issue angry statements and denials to the press.

Those solicited by the ring were of a different stripe. For them cost was no object, and the fact that buying a stolen masterpiece was flagrantly illegal only added to its desirability. What if the famous portrait had to be hidden from all eyes, enjoyed only by the purchaser and one or two confidants? What if nobody else knew the true facts? All of that simply spiced the venture with a bit of risk and added to the joy of secret ownership.

After some intense weeks of travel and activity, the Marqués and his two partners achieved their aim: verbal "contracts" were made with six potential buyers (their identities never revealed) and each assumed that he was the one and only bargainer. Then, in late summer of that year, Valfierno returned to Paris, where Perugia and the Lancelottis were waiting.

It was time now for the final act in the drama. The plan had been structured with the symmetry and precision of a Bach fugue, and all that remained was the actual theft of the *Mona Lisa*. If this formidable maneuver succeeded it would set off an uproar and create the right psychological atmosphere. This was the fulcrum on which everything balanced. Without it, the swindlers owned six nice copies of the *Gioconda* worth a few hundred dollars each, but after the robbery and the resulting publicity they could dispose of these same "masterpieces" for a fortune.

Though the Marqués had no way of anticipating it, his ingenious scenario was later to develop an unexpected hitch.

PART THREE

The Reaction

> But what shall we say of the guard that
> watches the gates of the Louvre? There is not
> even one guard per gallery. . . . The Louvre
> is less well protected than a Spanish museum.
>
> —GUILLAUME APOLLINAIRE,
> *article in* L'Intransigeant

12

ON BLACK TUESDAY, August 22, three different men in Paris were coping with anxieties involving the *Mona Lisa*. Louis Beroud, the young artist, was hurrying to the Louvre, intent on finishing his painting in the Salon Carré and selling it quickly. Vincenzo Perugia had reported to work as usual and now was trying to keep a normal façade despite mixed feeling of elation and fear. And at his hotel the Marqués de Valfierno was worriedly leafing through the morning newspapers.

The con man's vexation kept growing: a full day had passed since the theft, but there was still no mention in the press. Valfierno's mind was sufficiently devious to conjure up all sorts of obstacles. Were Théophile Homolle and the others planning to neutralize the robbery with a ruse of their own? They could, for instance, quietly substitute a duplicate portrait—one which they might have kept on hand for just such an emergency—and say no more about it, at least for the present. On the other hand, years earlier there had been certain rumors that *La Joconde* had been stolen. It had turned out to be a newspaper hoax, soon discredited; but did the officials at that time decide to put the real *Mona Lisa* in storage and leave a good facsimile in its place? Had he gone to all this trouble and expense to steal a decoy?

Despite these thoughts the Marqués had no real cause for concern, since the drama at the museum was unfolding with its own crazy logic and precision. At eleven that morn-

ing, while Valfierno sipped a *tisane* in the hotel lounge,
the truth had begun to dawn on Beroud and the guard
Poupardin as they stared at the empty space on the wall.
At that point *La Joconde* had been absent for some twenty-
seven hours. In the context of the Louvre's informality,
everyone assumed that the picture had been removed for
a legitimate reason and nobody thought of checking further.

Even Georges Picquet, the redoubtable head custodian, had been lulled into indifference. Police learned,
in the subsequent investigation, that at about 8:30 on
Monday morning Picquet and a few of his men had walked
through the Carré and noticed that the *Mona Lisa* was no
longer there. But he wasn't troubled. "Ha, look," he said,
"they've taken it away for protection, so none of us will try
to steal it." They all had a nice hearty laugh over the idea,
then went back to work.

So it wasn't until after 11 A.M. Tuesday that, pressured
by Beroud, Poupardin finally checked with the photo
studio and hurried to spread the alarm. His boss, the chief
of guards, quickly informed the curator of the Egyptian
collection, Georges Bénédite (Homolle was on vacation
and Bénédite was next in command), who telephoned
Louis Lepine, prefect of the Paris police. M. Lepine, a
legendary figure described by an associate as "a very small
man with a white beard who invariably wore a bowler hat
and an old-fashioned morning coat," rushed a corps of
gendarmes and detectives to the museum; he also notified
the Sûreté Nationale and the French Minister of the
Interior, then hurried to the Louvre to take charge
personally.

Hoping to avoid too much attention, the police spent
time quietly probing; but at 3 P.M. Lepine ordered them
to clear all the galleries and lock the exit doors, and the
search began in earnest. New visitors were turned away
with a cover story that a large water pipe had broken,
requiring emergency repairs; the police also put a squad on

the roof in case the thieves were still in hiding and tried
to evade their net.

For the next few hours, the Corinthian façade of the
vast building cloaked much urgent hurrying and scurrying
as a hundred hand-picked men explored stairways, halls,
storerooms and galleries. This initial search was superficial
by necessity, since it would have taken weeks to properly
check every inch of the museum, but during the afternoon
the hunters came across the frame and the shadow box
which Perugia had abandoned in the stairwell. Of *La
Joconde* and her abductors there was, of course, not the
slightest trace.

Meanwhile rumors circulated and a puzzled crowd
began to gather outside the main gates. The crowd grew in
size and was soon joined by a large number of reporters.
That afternoon, in the 5 P.M. edition of *Le Temps,* a small
paragraph appeared referring to the rumors, but the item
was placed inconspicuously. Then, at 5:30, M. Bénédite
made an official statement to the waiting newsmen. The
unhappy curator announced, *"La Joconde* is gone. So far
we have not the slightest clue as to the perpetrator of the
crime. . . . Yesterday was cleaning day and the museum
was closed to the public. Thus no one noticed the absence
of the picture. This morning the guard of the Salon Carré,
where the painting hung, noticed its disappearance and
attributed it to the negligence of the official photographer,
who often takes it up to his own studio and returns it the
next morning before the gates open to the public."

The statement said that, after the loss was discovered,
M. Lepine sent in an "army of detectives" who in due time
found the hidden picture frame. Bénédite concluded, "The
frame bore no marks of violence. The thief or thieves
evidently took plenty of time for the operation of dis-
mounting the picture, and discarded the frame as too
bulky. How he or they came or left is a mystery."

At that point the curator escaped from the barrage of

startled comments and questions and hastily retreated to
his office. Tuesday, which had been a long one for the
directors of the Louvre, ended on a note of doom and fore-
boding; and on Wednesday morning, August 23, the
bombshell which Valfierno had been awaiting exploded
in full force.

13

THE EDITORS of *Le Matin* announced the news with a
giant one-word banner head: *"INIMAGINABLE!"*

Other morning newspapers headlined Gallic cries
such as *"Inexplicable!" "Incroyable!"* and *"Effarant!,"* and
one caption in large letters declared: "You Have to Repeat
It to Yourself Ten Times Over in Order to Believe It!"
For the people of Paris the loss was indeed incredible and
bewildering; the absolutely impossible had happened, no
more logical than if the Arc de Triomphe had been flung
into the Seine. That day Parisians spoke of little else.
Gathered in cafés and bistros, in shops and tree-lined
squares, clustered around bookstalls on the Quai Voltaire,
the newspaper kiosks and the ubiquitous *pissotières,* they
argued, questioned and theorized.

Meanwhile the news had been instantly picked up by
the wire services and flashed around the world. Hundreds
of papers in Europe and America featured the scandal, and
Wednesday's front page story in *The New York Times,*
sent by special cable, began:

"LA GIOCONDA" IS
STOLEN IN PARIS

Impossible as it may seem, it is a fact that Leonardo
da Vinci's masterpiece, the "Mona Lisa," was stolen

yesterday from the Louvre, where it had been exhibited in the famous Salon Carré for the last five
years.

With France's Moroccan crisis in mind, the *Times* added
that the news caused such a sensation "that Parisians for
the time being have forgotten the rumors of war."

Eduardo de Valfierno, his anxieties at rest, savored
these reports and reactions—all he could have hoped for.
He was particularly charmed by a comment in *Le Figaro*:

> "La Joconde," by Leonardo da Vinci, has dis-
> appeared. This surpasses the imagination. Such an
> occurrence appears at first so enormous that one is
> tempted to laugh about it as though it were a bad
> joke . . . But since it has disappeared, perhaps forever,
> one must speak of this familiar face, whose memory
> will pursue us, filling us with regret in the same way
> that we speak of a person who died in a stupid
> accident . . .

The reporter, pursuing his metaphor, then went on to
write an obituary of the "deceased" portrait.

Other newspapers, less philosophical, lashed out at the
Louvre's poor security, the laxity of the police, and the
bungling of a bureaucracy which was, according to *Le
Temps*, guilty of "sabotaging our national collections."

After scanning all these reports, the Marqués sat down
at a writing desk, scribbled a cryptic note to V. Perugia
at 5 Rue de l'Hôpital-St.-Louis, then went upstairs to plan
his final visit to New York.

Now that the queen had been removed from the board
it was time for the end game, and Chaudron's forged panels
could be duly delivered and paid for; a welcome prospect,
since Valfierno's funds were beginning to run low. But
there were still some risks involved. To convince his buyers
that the portrait had been successfully "smuggled" out of

France, a few weeks would have to pass, and during that time the police might somehow recover the painting and arrest Perugia. If this were to happen *after* the fakes had been disposed of, it wouldn't necessarily be serious; he could always soothe his clients with a trumped-up story, and at any rate they would then be accessories. But if the real *Mona Lisa* appeared now it would wreck the whole timetable and cause tedious complications. The Marqués disliked tedious complications and had done all he could to avoid them. The forgeries were on the other side of the Atlantic. The genuine portrait was hidden in the safest of all places—the shadow of the Louvre, where no one would think of searching. Perugia and the others, with their freedom at stake, could be relied on to act with caution. So Valfierno had no choice but to be patient a little while longer.

"For the next few weeks," he observed to an anxious Chaudron, "we must put our faith in the incompetence of the French police."

14

HISTORICALLY THE YEAR 1911 was commonplace and, like all commonplace years, filled with its own small astonishments. It was the year in which Paris fashion designers scandalized Europe by introducing trousers for women, called "divided skirts." In America it was the year Henry Ford replaced the wooden bodies of his Model T autos with metal ones. That February, Vivien Gould, granddaughter of the fabled Jay Gould, married a British peer, the fifth Lord Decies; and it was reported that over two hundred seamstresses worked on the bride's trousseau.

Carrie Nation, scourge of the great American thirst, died that June at the age of sixty-six. Later in the month came the glittering coronation of England's King George V, a pageant and spectacle unequaled in all of Europe. In July, Thomas Edison predicted in a speech that aviation would put an end to war, since its awesome powers would act as a "psychological deterrent" to aggressor nations. As part of his Friars Club initiation, a young composer named Irving Berlin dashed off a ditty, "Alexander's Ragtime Band," later to become the greatest of ragtime's hits. Dancing in America was all the rage, and everyone knew the bunny hug and the triple Boston, but a new routine, the tango, hadn't quite caught on, *The New York Times* reported, since most dancers found it "a little risqué."

In 1911 there was a serious earthquake in Mexico, Italy went briefly to war with Turkey, Ty Cobb of the Detroit Tigers led both leagues with a batting average of .420, and explorer Roald Amundsen, using skis and dog teams, won his race against Robert Scott to become the first man to reach the South Pole. But in terms of the unforeseen and unexpected, no event anywhere that year could match the disappearance of the First Lady of France from her place on a wall of the Louvre.

For weeks following the incredible theft, the shock waves rumbled throughout the country. A distinguished jurist, Henri Drioux, was appointed *juge d'instruction* by Premier Joseph Caillaux to conduct an official investigation. The Undersecretary for Fine Arts, Dujardin-Beaumetz, rushed back to Paris from his vacation in Carcassonne. Museum director Homolle and Paul Leprieur, the Louvre's curator of paintings, also cut their holidays short and hurried home. Feelings among Parisians spanned the emotional spectrum from anguish to alarm, dismay to disbelief, fury to ridicule; and the editors of the magazine *L'Illustration* cried indignantly, "What audacious criminal, what mystifier, what maniac collector, what insane lover, has committed this abduction?"

As the investigation got under way, rumors were re-

peated with great relish and the police were deluged with
tips and clues. Acting on an anonymous phone call,
they picked up two "suspicious" German artists but
soon released them. One informant described a stout
bearded man with a painting wrapped in a blanket who on
the morning of the theft was seen racing for the 7:47 A.M.
train to Bordeaux. Attempts to trace this gentleman along
the route of the train got nowhere. A teenage boy reported
seeing several "shifty-looking" men hurrying across the
Quai de Javel, carrying a mysterious covered panel; and an
antiques dealer near the Louvre told of being approached
by a poorly dressed, nervous man who offered to sell him a
"very rare portrait of a noblewoman."

The stories continued, and *La Joconde*'s kidnappers
were variously reported to be in Le Havre and Marseilles,
in Dijon, Reims, Rouen and Nantes. A nebulous "Baron
S.," supposedly a wealthy art lover, figured briefly in the
news reports, as did one Étienne Flagy, a self-described
homme des lettres. For the sum of 200,000 francs, M. Flagy
offered to reveal "the true facts" to the authorities, but
when he was confronted by the police his mind drew a
blank. A young waiter in a café, Armand Gueneschan, also
demanded 200,000 francs in return for key information:
though not involved in the theft, he claimed that he knew
just where the *Mona Lisa* was hidden. If there was no payment within two days, he warned, the panel would be destroyed; then "it will not be the painting which is returned,
but the ashes." Gendarmes questioned the waiter for
twenty-four hours, searched his room carefully and concluded that he was harmless though quite demented.

Later two swimmers at Dinard, off the Brittany coast,
turned in a note which they had found sealed in a small
bottle. The message, signed "B.T.S.," claimed that *La
Joconde* had been drowned at sea, but it soon proved to be
a hoax.

Another floating message was found by a boatman on the Seine, near the Pont des Arts. Fishing the bottle from the water, he found a scribbled fragment inside: "Don't bother looking for the Mona Lisa any longer. It's at my place, Rue du Pélican. Since I couldn't get rid of it, have no money and am wretched, I destroyed it, hacked it to pieces. I am going to kill myself." The unsigned note was, according to *La Patrie*, "assuredly the work of a madman or hoaxer." As expected, nobody in the Rue du Pélican knew anything about the matter; but it did supply local residents with hours of enjoyable gossip and speculation.

During all this, the Prefecture of Police and the Sûreté (France's F.B.I.) were trying desperately to locate the elusive *Joconde*. The borders of the country were virtually sealed off, with roadblocks and rail checkpoints everywhere; and baggage, particularly of those leaving France, was dumped and searched. On August 29 the steamship *Kaiser Wilhelm II* docked in New York and was scoured by detectives from prow to rudder posts. The French liner *La Champagne*, en route to South America, was ransacked. Next came the *Oceanic*, the dowager of England's fleet of luxury liners, which was all but turned inside out at her dock in Cherbourg. Police in Bordeaux also quarantined and searched the steamship *Cordillère*, perhaps in connection with the bearded mystery man previously seen running for the Bordeaux train.

None of this prodding and probing brought any results except to discomfort large numbers of transatlantic passengers and frightened a few amateur artists with souvenir paintings in their luggage. By now the search (and the rumors) had grown worldwide, and while the real *Mona Lisa*, still wrapped in Perugia's tunic, reposed in a dingy room not far from the Louvre, it was reportedly seen in Argentina and Germany, Belgium and Brazil, England, the United States, Italy, Russia, Peru and Japan.

At the museum the investigation went into high gear; everyone who worked in the building was fingerprinted and scores of employees were interrogated, among them Poupardin, the chief of guards, Sauvet the plumber, and the custodian Picquet. The laborer who saw Perugia toss the doorknob away had by this time come forward, and the doorknob was found still lying in the ditch. Soon the investigators were able to piece together a few definite facts, including the hour of the robbery and the probable route followed by the thieves. The Prefecture then appealed to the people of Paris, "in the hope of reaching anyone who had noticed in the neighborhood of the Louvre, at around 7:30 on Monday morning, a man of medium height, strongly built, forty to fifty years old, dressed in a dark suit and a straw hat and carrying a package that looked like a panel of wood . . ."

The police had gotten his age wrong (Perugia was a good bit younger), but the other details were fairly accurate, and Vincenzo drew some comfort from the fact that the description could apply as well to half the men in Paris. During those days the carpenter/house painter handled himself with surprising skill. He reported to work every day as usual and was able (due perhaps to sheer lack of imagination) to stay remarkably calm and cool. He also spent time planning how, when things settled down, he would spend the money given him by the *signore,* which he had carefully hidden.

Now and then in the evening, Perugia would join his friends Vincent and Michele Lancelotti at a bistro near the brothers' rooms on the Rue Bichat; and over a few beers they would listen to the latest crop of rumors: *La Joconde* had been thrown away on a garbage dump; it had been deliberately sabotaged with acid and would never be seen again; a Chicago meat packer had just bought it for millions of dollars; the thieves had stolen a forgery, since the real *Mona Lisa* had never been in the museum to begin with; a lovesick young artist, infatuated with the lady's smile, had hidden the painting in his attic; the panel had been accidentally destroyed in a fire, and the "theft" was simply a cover-up; the whole thing was a stunt by newspapermen, to show how easy it was to steal from the Louvre . . .

As each of these wild stories was loudly presented and eagerly examined, Perugia and his friends would listen, shake their heads, and roll their eyes in sanctimonious disbelief at the deviousness of the modern world.

While that trio carefully avoided the limelight, other players were caught up in it. Poupardin, Louis Beroud and to a lesser extent Georges Picquet became minor folk heroes, interviewed and quoted in the daily tabloids. As museum employees, both the guard and the custodian were under a cloud; but the artist basked in his notoriety and enjoyed his new reputation as "the man who alerted the Louvre."

In actual fact, that tiny distinction really belonged not to Louis Beroud but to a young American painter, Orland Campbell. In 1963, a letter-cum-memoir was sent by Campbell to a friend who forwarded it to Theodore Rousseau, curator of paintings at the Metropolitan Museum of Art. Rousseau in turn passed the interesting curiosity on to Germain Bazin, then one of the Louvre's directors. Orland Campbell's letter described his experiences that crucial Tuesday, while he was visiting France:

> It was the hot summer of 1911 and I was a student of art in Paris for the first time. Almost every day found me in the painting galleries of the Louvre Museum, each day beginning where I had left off before. So—it happened that closing time, one day, found me standing for the first time before the Mona

> Lisa who . . . did not hang in the very long Grande
> Galerie where we saw her recently but, I believe, to
> the right of the entrance door in one of the smaller
> exhibition rooms . . .

Campbell, like many others, was entranced by the
portrait and stayed there that Sunday until closing. And
when the Louvre reopened on Tuesday:

> I walked hurriedly to the distant room where I
> had left off before, but—where was the Mona Lisa?
> Where she had been, there was nothing—just empty
> wall! I looked for a guard but at that early hour there
> were no humans in sight, and when a guard was finally
> found he knew nothing of the empty wall, but went
> with me to see for himself. Very puzzled, he shook
> his head, looking hard at the bare wall, then—with a
> shrug, "Perhaps the photographer has her?"
> That is the story, and that day at the Louvre
> passed without event until about three in the after-
> noon when a cordon of guards, walking abreast with
> arms interlocked . . . , swept the length of the Grande
> Galerie. That was the day the Musée du Louvre
> closed early. But it was from the papers that we
> learned the story of the theft . . .

It can be assumed that the guard queried by young Campbell was the venerable Poupardin, who a short while later
was to sound the alarm and shatter the serenity of Paris.

Orland Campbell, for years a resident of New York's
Hotel des Artistes, died in 1972. During his life he created
successful portraits of American celebrities and social
figures; in 1959 he also found and restored Gilbert Stuart's
notable portrait of Thomas Jefferson, later placed in the
State Department Building in Washington, D.C. To those
achievements must now be added the fact that he was the
very first to point out, though in vain, that the invincible
Louvre was minus one of its masterpieces.

Meanwhile the round-the-clock hunt for that master-piece continued; by now Paris had become an enormous posse with everyone involved, and as the tempo of the search increased it attracted strange participants.

15

The heavyset fleshy woman, a dozen bracelets jangling on her wrists, leaned back in the big chair and closed her eyes while a group of devotees joined in a silent circle. In the dim Montmartre studio the woman's body grew rigid, her pudgy fingers clawed at the armrests, she began to make eerie moaning sounds ...

That fall and winter, many such scenes were being enacted all over Paris. Seances were taken very seriously in those years, and spiritualists did a lively business with their assorted table rappings, blasts on floating trumpets, the creation of "ectoplasm" (a few yards of gauze dipped in phosphorescent paint and waved in a darkened room) and scores of incredibly banal messages supposedly from loved ones who had "passed to the other side."

These practitioners were soon enlisted in the hunt, and *Le Matin* offered a reward of five thousand francs (equal then to about $1,000) to any occultist, medium or clair-voyant who could help to recover the *Mona Lisa* "by means of the Beyond."

Drawn by this prize, not to mention possible reams of free publicity, the psychics of Paris responded with zest. Witches and high priestesses, oracles and fortunetellers, astrologers, palmists, wizards, warlocks, crystal gazers and tarot readers all girded themselves for the search. With spells and incantations, charts, charms, talismans and familiars, the magi tried to conjure up answers to the growing mystery. But output far exceeded usefulness, and the resulting predictions set new highs for inaccuracy. Most of these bizarre "psychic messages" were faithfully reported in the press, and a few proved of some interest. Among those on record:

Mme. Henri, known as the Witch of Mont Ventoux, stated simply, "The painting is far away—the thief is here."

Mme. de Mozard claimed that while in a trance she had seen the *Mona Lisa* in Germany. To retrieve the portrait, she added cryptically, "one must act with mystery and discretion."

Mme. Loni-Feignez of the Rue Pierre-Levée, more generous with details, told reporters that three men were involved—two short and one tall. The tall thief, the only Frenchman in the group, was the one who had actually unhooked the painting from the wall. The accomplices, she said, acted on behalf of a rich, fanatic art lover who lived in a western suburb of Paris and who often came to the Louvre to contemplate the da Vinci masterpiece. The painting itself could be found near the Hôtel de Ville, Paris's City Hall (a close guess, since this was within a few blocks of Séguenot's garret on the Rue St.-Merri).

A certain Mme. Siddhis felt that the *Mona Lisa* would return "of her own accord" to the Louvre, but that she had been damaged.

M. Binou, an amateur clairvoyant and professional violin repairer, disagreed. The painting, he said, "is at sea, and due to anchor in New York in five or six days."

Mlle. Symiane Mina saw the abductor hiding in a "sordid attic." In a burst of Dickensian imagery she described him as a "bespectacled Württemburger" who wore a goatee. He and another German were now busy repairing the portrait. Mlle. Symiane said that if she were allowed to physically touch the iron hooks where the painting had hung, she could easily name the thief, but permission to do this had been denied her. "Those who know," she added darkly, "will read between the lines."

Mme. Stahl, director of an institute for "magnetic research," called on her favorite sensitive, one Mlle. Edmée, to help solve the case. Under hypnosis the young woman divined that several people were involved, one a heavyset man, fiftyish, who was "well known," another, who actually removed the painting, thirty-five years old and tall. In her trance, Mlle. Edmée saw the *Mona Lisa* tucked away "in a garden, by a door." Mme. Stahl then predicted that soon there would be no more discussion of the theft, for "sinister political reasons."

Mme. Alpaïde Darmourde took a similar line. Claiming, with no undue modesty, to "know it all," she refused to say anything because the theft involved "the most significant personalities of our time." Furthermore, "the slightest disclosure would bring the worst misfortune on the country." In a later reversal (brought on perhaps by thoughts of *Le Matin*'s reward), Mme. Darmourde announced that she would break the story open in precisely forty-eight hours, but the revelation never took place.

A psychic named Mme. Elise was grossly incorrect and refreshingly blunt; the portrait, she announced with grief, "has been destroyed."

Mme. Albano de Siva was more sanguine. By studying the positions of the planets she deduced the time of the theft as Monday, the twenty-first, at 7:53 A.M. The perpetrator was a man "interested in restoring ruins, and determined to beautify cities with works of art." She pictured him as middle-aged, wearing a reddish beard, and with two accomplices. The police had missed an excellent chance on August 27, she said, of capturing this master thief, but he had slipped through their fingers and was now in the south of France. Mme. de Siva added rather bafflingly that "he belongs to the opposition."

Finally a Mme. de Poncey, electing to cover all possible bases, asserted, "This theft is a question of internal or external politics—but definitely a state secret which will never be divulged."

With Germany as France's historic rival and with the friction in North Africa uppermost in people's minds, it isn't surprising that many clairvoyants decided the thieves were Germans. Most of them sensed, which was true enough, that the painting hadn't left France. They also felt, as did the police, that more than one person was involved; and the irrepressible Mme. de Siva made a fairly good guess as to the correct hour of the crime. Outside of those minor points, not a single communiqué "from the beyond" proved of any help whatsoever in the quest for the *Mona Lisa.*

The editors of *Le Matin,* their reward unclaimed, took note of a distressing fact. "None of these intimates of the unknown," they grumbled, "can come up with a story of the crime which concurs with any other." And an analyst for *Le Figaro,* reviewing all the messages, wrote, "Alas, in this affair the clairvoyants may see clearer than the police," then added as an afterthought, "but not by much."

To Judge Drioux, Louis Lepine and other bloodhounds it was obvious that, for help in tracing *La Joconde,* they would have to look elsewhere than the spirit world.

16

THE PUBLISHERS of *Le Matin* weren't the only ones in those weeks to dangle rewards.

A distinguished society of art patrons known as Les Amis du Louvre offered 25,000 francs (about $5,000) for information leading to the recovery of the painting. The magazine *L'Illustration* announced a reward of 10,000 francs for productive clues, and 40,000 to anyone who actually delivered the portrait to its offices. *Paris-Journal* upped this to 50,000 francs, with anonymity guaranteed and no questions asked. A number of wealthy citizens also pledged sums as prizes and inducements.

But as the days passed without results, hope slowly turned to uncertainty, and uncertainty to despair. *Le Figaro* reported:

> The police have pursued a fruitless inquiry. They have found no suspects. However, it seems that the mysterious thief was familiar with the Lourve or had knowing accomplices . . . the thief is no hoaxer; he knew the Louvre, its weaknesses and negligence.

Where was the elusive *Mona Lisa*? Everyone had a pet theory as to why it had been taken. Louis Lepine suspected sabotage by vengeful museum employees; there was also a possibility, he said, "that *La Joconde* was stolen by someone who plans to make a profit by blackmailing the government." Leprieur, the curator of paintings, felt that it was taken "by someone who intends to return a good copy later." The editors of *Paris-Match* asked cynically, "Are we dealing with a real theft or a practical joke?" They thought the portrait could have been kidnapped by a sensation-seeking journalist who was after a big story; it had to be a stunt, they said, and the masterpiece would be returned later with lots of fanfare. "How," they added, "can a real thief hope to profit financially from a picture so universally known?"

There were also, then as now, various conspiracy theories: the whole episode was a political device, a manipulation by Caillaux's government to distract people from the troubles in Morocco. And one faction insisted doggedly that the painting hadn't been stolen at all—that it was a ruse by the directors of the Louvre to gain publicity and boost attendance!

Curiously, one theory—the least credited of all—came closest to the truth. It was advanced by Joseph Reinach, a prominent journalist, member of the French Chamber of Deputies and one of the leaders of Les Amis du Louvre. In an interview, M. Reinach pointed out that there were a number of fine copies of *La Joconde* in existence which dated from da Vinci's own era. What if one of these old versions had fallen into the hands of thieves? They might plan someday to return the stolen picture to the Louvre, but meanwhile, thought Reinach, they could "sell the copy of the *Mona Lisa* to a millionaire collector, less skilled than the conservators, explaining that the picture they had for sale was the original, and that the Louvre possessed only a copy."

This concept found little support, though it touched surprisingly on aspects of Valfierno's swindle; and at the very moment that Reinach was being brushed aside by the investigators, the Marqués and his partners were beginning to contact their clients in America.

By early September, Drioux had finished his investigation and the Louvre was reopened to the public. Thousands flocked to the Salon Carré (including many who had never set foot there when the *Mona Lisa* was in residence) to stare at the four hooks, now more naked than ever; and a number of visitors brought bouquets of roses which they quietly placed on the floor. *La Patrie,* hunting for a wisp of silver lining on the clouds of gloom, reported that at any rate "Parisians have discovered the existence of the Louvre because of the theft of the *Mona Lisa.*"

But the mood of the city wasn't somber for long. Roy McMullen, art historian and former editor of the Paris *Herald Tribune,* wrote that as time passed the original shock was replaced by "humor, faddism and hucksterism," and soon there was a brisk sale of songs, poems and post-cards dealing with the lost madonna. One ballad was plain-

tively called "Have You Seen Her—La Joconde?" Another
song to the tune of "Auprès de Ma Blonde" was titled
"Mona Lisa on a Spree," and asked, now that she had fled
the Louvre, *"est elle à Douvres, New York ou Pékin?"*

Somebody inevitably wrote a "Gioconda Waltz," and
theatrical performers, among them the famed Mistinguett,
did tableaus and "impersonations" of *La Joconde.*
McMullen reports that Paris's cabaret entertainers, searching for the vanished smile, sang an aria, "No, it isn't you
. . . it isn't your face," with the melody borrowed from
Gounod's *Faust.*

Several newspapers printed a retouched photo of the
Cathedral of Notre-Dame with a tower missing, and under
it the caption "CAN THIS HAPPEN NEXT?" A cartoon in the
English magazine *Punch* showed the *Venus de Milo* reading a headline about the robbery. "Paris will have something left at any rate," she muses. "The thief isn't born
who can lift *me.*" And the staff of *Paris-Journal* suggested
that a notice be posted in all French museums which
should read:

In the Interest of Art
And for the Safeguarding of the Precious Objects,
THE PUBLIC
Is Requested to Be Good Enough to
WAKE THE GUARDS
If They Are Found to Be Asleep.

Satire and ridicule helped to focus attention on the
glaring deficiencies of the Louvre's security. Though exact
figures vary in different reports, there were apparently no
more than ten or twelve guards *in the entire building* on
the day Perugia and his friends strolled off with their
fabulous prize. According to *Le Temps,* two of these had
been assigned that Monday to cleaning details, while
several others were helping to move a collection of sculp-

tures; which left an absurdly small crew (including the guard at the Visconti Gate) to protect vast acres of precious art and to keep an eye on a dozen possible exit doors.

In addition, the security forces of the country had long been at odds with each other. The Paris Prefecture of Police, a highly independent body, had authority over the city and the suburbs. The Sûreté Nationale (comparable to the F.B.I. and Britain's Scotland Yard) was responsible for security and crime prevention throughout the country. As is often the case, there was great jealousy between these groups and cooperation was kept to a minimum. Jean Belin, who later became a commissioner of the Sûreté, confided in his memoirs, "The rivalry that existed between our two principal police organizations was such that time and again their men handled the same case in direct competition, and quite frequently they would try to discredit each other." Valuable clues were sometimes withheld by the two bureaus and files on criminals were exchanged rarely, if at all.

M. Belin pointed out another scandalous fact: "One way in which rivalry between the two camps was often expressed was by arresting each other's informers. To do so was to hamstring the activities and effectiveness of the officers concerned, and unfortunately this sort of thing happened only too often."

Given that kind of rancor, there's little wonder that the Sûreté and the police outdid each other in trying to shift the blame, while angry charges and countercharges ricocheted through the offices of the Palais de Justice, the Conciergerie and the Chamber of Deputies. Then, in the midst of this teapot tempest, a flash of good news arrived: the sleuths had struck gold. Lepine and the others learned with relief that Alphonse Bertillon, the great French criminologist, had succeeded in obtaining a perfect thumbprint from the glass case abandoned in the stairwell—a print obviously left by one of the gang while removing the portrait.

If Valfierno or Perugia had known of this find (then kept secret) they would have been greatly alarmed, and with reason. Vincenzo Perugia, as noted earlier, had been arrested twice before by the Paris police: in June 1908 he was picked up on a charge of attempted robbery, but released after twenty-four hours; in February 1909 he was again arrested, during an argument with a streetwalker, and given an eight-day sentence for illegal possession of a weapon (a knife). Though the offenses were minor, Perugia was fingerprinted on both occasions, so the police had *two* sets of his prints already on file; and at that logical point the case could well have been solved, the guilty ones arrested, and *La Joconde* escorted in style back to the Carré.

But once again, the most unlikely of circumstances protected the little band and rescued Valfierno's threatened enterprise.

M. Bertillon's vast rogue's gallery on the Île de la Cité held the records of some 750,000 criminals and police cases (Perugia's among them), all carefully classified. The lone print which the experts had found on the glass pane was from someone's left thumb. (This was easy to determine: on a print made by a right thumb, the delicate curves, or whorls, go in a clockwise pattern; on left thumbprints they turn counterclockwise.) But in Bertillon's cataloguing system—at that time by far the most efficient anywhere—only prints of the *right* thumb were used for classification! Incredibly, no prints of left hands were kept on file, so, even with this solid clue in their possession, the police had absolutely no way of checking it with the records.

At that time, hundreds of people employed at the Louvre—guards, laborers, administrators, curators, clerks

—were questioned and fingerprinted, and these prints were systematically matched against the thumbprint on the glass; yet for some reason (though he was later questioned by a police inspector) nobody thought to take Perugia's finger-prints anew, nor was his name on the list compiled by M. Hamard of the Sûreté for screening by Bertillon's print experts. The carpenter was no longer connected with the museum and hadn't worked there for months, but still the oversight points up the bad coordination between the bureaus dealing with the crime. At that critical point the authorities had Perugia under their thumb, so to speak, but weren't aware of their good luck.

Some years later *Petit Parisien,* reviewing the story, pointed out how simple it would have been to arrest Perugia a few days after the theft of *La Joconde.* The editors reported:

> A preliminary list of 257 people was first of all communicated to the Criminal Records office; a second list, with names of people who had been doing various jobs, followed. All these people's prints were scrupulously compared with that lifted from the glass; but those of Perugia were notable by their absence. Only he had been forgotten!

The newspaper added that the Criminal Records Office was "completely unaware that Vincenzo Perugia had once been employed at the Louvre."

The museum's only real witness, Sauvet the plumber, had also been put to work during the investigation. Sitting in a musty office, he shuffled through hundreds of photo-graphs in hopes of identifying the mysterious workmen he had seen in the stairwell. But as Sauvet explained to the police, the light was very dim, and at the time he had barely glanced at them. Dressed in standard white tunics, the group had blended facelessly with all the other museum workers. In any event, having the plumber screen pictures proved fruitless, since no photos of Perugia or the Lance-lottis had been included.

Such gaffes seemed almost to fit a pattern—a pattern which will be examined shortly. The significant fact is that, from the moment Valfierno's plan was launched, fortune smiled on the thieves and mishaps plagued the investi-gators, all of which helped to shield the conspiracy. Again and again there were absurd blunders, failures and mis-adventures until at times the search for the *Mona Lisa* bordered on Keystone Kops or *opéra comique*.

One charade, not widely known, featured a brilliant poet and a young genius painter, both of whom would later become world famous. At that point Guillaume Apollinaire and Pablo Picasso were fairly obscure, but a twist of fate made them buffoons in the drama—a pair of dancing bears in the weirdest episode involving the lost portrait.

17

ON THE NIGHT of September 5, 1911, anyone strolling along the Quai de Conti or the Quai Malaquais on the left bank of the Seine might have seen two young men behaving somewhat furtively. The men, both in worn, vaguely bo-hemian clothes, had a cheap suitcase which they took turns in carrying, and as they sauntered west to the Pont de la Concorde, then doubled back, they glanced nervously over their shoulders and occasionally one or the other would stop to stare over the stone wall into the dark waters.

The suitcase which Apollinaire and Picasso dragged with them that night contained several priceless statuettes which had been stolen from the Louvre. Now, with all

Paris on the lookout for the kidnappers of *La Joconde* as
well as other art thieves, the friends had decided to get
rid of their incriminating statues by tossing them into the
river. However, they lost their nerve, the plan failed, and
they wound up, cold and exhausted, back in Picasso's studio
on the Boulevard de Clichy with the evidence—and their
troubles—still on their hands.

Picasso's anxious partner in this misadventure was
born in Rome in 1880, the illegitimate child of an im-
poverished woman who at one time had been a member
of the Polish nobility. Later, when Guillaume-Albert-
Wladimir-Alexandre Apollinaire de Kostrowitsky settled
with his mother in Paris, there were rumors (possibly
started by Apollinaire) that his father had been "at least
a cardinal and perhaps a pope."

In the early 1900s the flamboyant Guillaume epito-
mized Paris's thriving avant-garde—a successful poet,
editor, art critic, pamphleteer and spokesman-prophet for
the new school of Cubism. According to historian James
Mellow, "Florid in complexion, jut-jawed and with a regal
profile, Apollinaire cut an extraordinary figure in the
Parisian art world"; and Gertrude Stein, herself fast becoming a major cultural institution, found him "very
attractive and very interesting" and observed that "he had
a head like one of the late Roman emperors."

Along with Picasso, Matisse, Braque, Salmon, Juan
Gris, Max Jacob, the aged Henri Rousseau and others,
Apollinaire was a regular guest at Gertrude Stein's legendary Saturday-evening salons on the Rue de Fleurus. Here
he held forth with great zest, and his hostess wrote of him:
"Guillaume was extraordinarily brilliant and no matter
what subject was started, if he knew anything about it or
not, he quickly saw the whole meaning of the thing and
elaborated it by his wit and fancy . . ."

Apollinaire made it his business to know everyone in

Paris, and among his many acquaintances was a slightly mad young Belgian named Géry Pieret, a witty, itinerant, devil-may-care former boxer and sometime writer whose weakness for gambling left him congenitally short of ready cash. For a time, in 1907, Pieret acted as Apollinaire's secretary and general assistant. One day in the poet's studio, he turned to Apollinaire's mistress, the painter Marie Laurencin, and said, "Marie, I'm going to the Louvre; is there anything I can bring you?" Laurencin, assuming that he meant a large Paris department store called the Magasin du Louvre, thanked him and said that there really wasn't anything she needed at the moment. But Pieret was referring not to the *magasin* but to the *musée,* and much later, when the theft of *La Joconde* was making headlines, he sold his quixotic story to the newspaper *Paris-Journal.* In it, Pieret wrote that he first visited the Louvre in March 1907 merely to kill some time, with no thought of stealing anything. The idea seemed completely impossible to him, but he abruptly changed his mind:

> At about one o'clock I found myself in the gallery of Asiatic antiquities. A single guard was sitting motionless. I was about to climb the stairs leading to the floor above when I noticed a half-open door on my left. I had only to push it, and found myself in a room filled with hieroglyphs and Egyptian statues. . . . It was at that moment that I suddenly realized how easy it would be to pick up and take away almost any object of moderate size.

Pieret was wearing a roomy overcoat that afternoon, and his "natural slimness" made it possible for him to slip something under his coat and not attract any attention. After examining forty or fifty carved heads arranged on the dusty shelves, he chose one of a Phoenician woman, tucked it under his clothes and calmly walked out, asking directions from the dozing watchman. His confession in *Paris-Journal* went on:

> I sold the statue to a Parisian painter friend of mine. He gave me a little money—fifty francs, I think, which I lost the same night in a billiard parlor.
> "What of it?" I said to myself, "All Phoenicia is there for the taking."

Géry Pieret made other raids on the unguarded store-rooms of the Louvre, each time leaving with new treasures hidden in his clothing. At this point the facts grew contradictory. Picasso indicated that he bought two small Iberian heads, or masks, from Géry at Apollinaire's suggestion, and that he had no inkling they were stolen goods; but Fernande Olivier, then Picasso's mistress, has a different version. She says in her memoirs:

> Géry, whom Apollinaire had taken to see Picasso, had given the painter two quite beautiful little stone masks, without revealing where he had got them from. He had only said that they should not be exhibited too conspicuously. Picasso was enchanted, and he treasured these gifts and buried them at the very back of a cupboard.

Pieret then went off to seek his fortune in Mexico; several years went by, and Fernande said later, "We used to come across these little masterpieces occasionally if we were rumaging in the old Norman cupboard, but we never gave them a thought."

Whether they were purchases or gifts, it's evident that Picasso definitely knew of the illicit nature of his Iberian heads and took care to keep them hidden. Apollinaire had also received a primitive statuette from the generous Pieret, but despite his friend's warnings he proudly displayed it on his mantelpiece.

In 1911, the wanderer came back to Paris and, again

out of funds, resumed his little visits to the Louvre; but after a foray or two he decided to postpone all this until he could have functional clothing made—perhaps "a pair of leather cowboy trousers and some special suspenders." Pieret may have intended to pick the museum clean, but the shocking theft of the *Mona Lisa* in August put an end to his ambitions. It also brought Guillaume and Pablo face to face with disaster.

Eight days after the robbery in the Salon Carré, an unusual headline appeared in *Paris-Journal:* "A THIEF BRINGS US A STATUE STOLEN FROM THE LOUVRE! Curator Admits the Piece Is from the Museum."

The thief was Géry Pieret. With the Louvre—and Paris—in a turmoil over *La Joconde,* new raids were out of the question; so, making the best of this situation, the rash Belgian sold one of his statues, plus a full confession, to the press. *Paris-Journal* played up the story, taunting museum officials for their laxity and exhibiting the statuette in their front window. Crowds flocked to see it and the editors noted, "The realization that organized pillage of our museums indeed exists, as revealed with such perverse ingenuity by our thief, causes general stupefaction."

Stung by this, Lepine's investigators doubled their efforts. With the police now closing in on him, Pieret collected his money from *Paris-Journal* and skipped town; but his identity and his friends had become known—and the trail led straight to Apollinaire. He and Picasso were terrified; not only had they knowingly received stolen goods from Pieret but they were both aliens, subject to deportation. A panicky meeting at the painter's studio led to the decision to dump the hot statuettes, and Fernande Olivier recalls:

> Finally, after a hurried dinner and an interminable evening of waiting—for they had made up their minds to go that night and throw the suitcase into

the Seine—they left on foot at about midnight . . .
They returned at two in the morning, absolutely dog-
tired. They still had the suitcase and its contents.

The two men had wandered around anxiously, unable
to hit on the right moment or perhaps unwilling to carry
out the deed. According to Fernande they became paranoid
and thought they were being followed. "Their imagina-
tions," she wrote, "had dreamed up a thousand possible
occurrences, each more fantastic than the last. . . . I am sure
they were seeing themselves as characters in a play."

The poet and the artist undoubtedly enjoyed this
chance to dramatize themselves; neither of them knew
anything about cardplaying, but Fernande recalls that
while waiting for midnight and the crucial visit to the river
they "pretended to play cards, like gangsters."

The upshot was that Apollinaire spent a wretched
night at the studio and the next morning went to the offices
of *Paris-Journal* to turn over the stolen loot in return for
a promise of anonymity. In his memoirs Apollinaire claims
that it was Picasso himself who brought the statuettes
secretly to the newspaper; in either case the editors were
delighted to have a new scoop, which meant more scandal
and more circulation for *Paris-Journal*.

The statues were off their hands at last, but for
Guillaume it was too late. Anonymous tips and rumors
had reached the Prefecture linking the poet with the mysterious fugituve Géry Pieret; Apollinaire had also been
seen with Pieret at the railroad station, when the young
man was arranging to flee Paris. So it was simple enough
for the police, desperate for answers, to convince themselves
that Géry was connected with the robbery in the Salon
Carré and that his mentor, Apollinaire, was also involved.

On September 7 the unhappy poet was arrested, suspected of heading an "international gang of art thieves"
and of masterminding the heist of the *Mona Lisa*.
Guillaume, innocent of these charges, and until then an

incurable romantic, had a sudden rude awakening. "Abruptly," wrote biographer Antonia Vallentin, "the underworld lost its picturesque attractions for him as he found himself caught up in an implacable judiciary machine." Poor Apollinaire was plunged into fear and despair, but it didn't lessen his urge to self-dramatize; in an essay published later, he recalled: "From the moment the heavy gate of La Santé prison closed behind me, I had a sensation of death . . . it seemed to me . . . that I occupied a place situated outside of our world, and that I was going to my destruction."

No longer play-acting but experiencing the real thing, he was taken in handcuffs to Cell Number 15, and there

> I had to strip naked in the corridor and was searched.
> I was then locked up. I slept very little because of
> the electric light that is kept on all night in the cells.
> Everybody knows what prison life is like: a purgatory
> of boredom, where you are alone and yet constantly
> spied on.

From there he was marched to the Palais de Justice and for two days questioned by a stern magistrate. At first Guillaume showed bravado, denying any involvement with Pieret or the stolen goods; but his resolve crumbled under pressure and he wound up confessing to all sorts of outlandish charges—and also implicating others, including the worried Pablo.

Now it was Picasso's turn, and early one morning he too was escorted to the Prefecture by a uniformed policeman. Pierre Cabanne, in his biography of the famed painter, noted: "The meeting between Apollinaire and Pablo before the authorities was a disaster; both got confused and contradicted themselves and each other—for, both being foreigners, their main object was to avoid being deported." Picasso was in a state of panic, and Apollinaire, pale and disheveled from his prison stay, was in tears. According to some reports the painter was so distraught he actually denied even *knowing* Guillaume, but Fernande Olivier claims that this is a falsehood. "Far from betraying him," she says of Picasso, "that moment brought out the true strength of his friendship with Apollinaire."

The men pleaded innocence with regard to the *Mona Lisa,* and Olivier adds that apparently they "both wept before the judge, who was quite paternal and had some difficulty in maintaining his judicial severity in the face of their childish grief."

Through all the tears and emotion, it became obvious to the judge that the men had been unduly victimized; the statuettes had after all been recovered and there wasn't a shred of hard evidence connecting them to the greater theft in the Carré. Picasso was soon released, but was told not to leave the Paris jurisdiction for the present. Apollinaire now had the help and support of several prestigious lawyers, and after a final interrogation he was released on September 12. All charges against the poet were finally dismissed in January of the following year.

For both men the episode had been traumatic, though fortunately it ended without any real disasters or permanent scars. According to Fernande:

> The whole affair was shelved and forgotten after a time; but for many weeks afterward Picasso and Apollinaire still thought they were being shadowed. Picasso would go out only at night in a taxi, and even then he used to switch cabs in order to put his "pursuers" off the scent.

In due course the memory of the trauma faded; Picasso stopped glancing nervously over his shoulder every time he walked along the Rue Ravignan, and Guillaume gradually overcame his depression, throwing himself into his work in an effort to regain the literary status he'd lost during the Louvre scandal. As for Pieret, according to Apollinaire he was arrested in Cairo, tried at the end of 1913 and later acquitted. Guillaume had no ill will toward his former secretary and was pleased at the outcome of Pieret's case. "The poor fellow," he wrote, "was crazy rather than a criminal; the courts must have thought so, too."

Other famous personalities were later caught in *La Joconde*'s web, but Apollinaire could claim one dubious distinction: he was, as he remarked to friends, the only person formally arrested in France in connection with the theft of the *Mona Lisa*.

18

"*L'Affaire* Apollinaire" caused a great furor, further embarrassed the police and added to the pressure to find scapegoats. The country's most prized painting had been brazenly snatched, no one could produce any clues—somebody had to take the blame.

Soon after Drioux's report went to Premier Caillaux and the French Cabinet, Théophile Homolle was fired as director of national museums and head curator of the Louvre. Various guards and staff members, including Picquet, were officially reprimanded and ordered to appear before a disciplinary board. In the Chamber of Deputies so much angry criticism was heaped on Dujardin-Beaumetz, the Undersecretary for Fine Arts, that he was forced to resign—a distinct loss to the art world, since he was a particularly gifted and sensitive administrator.

New rules for the Louvre were also set up. From now on, nobody would be allowed to touch or move a work of art without written authority. Public visiting hours were shortened, to permit better use of the available men. New guards were added. Some of the exit doors were permanently closed and the rest were closely monitored. Guard dogs were brought in, to help patrol the building at night. None of this belated effort helped in any way to clear up the mystery, but it did improve the museum's flimsy security.

As for Valfierno and his accomplices, they followed these matters with much interest. Vincenzo Perugia was still unaware of the real scope and nature of the swindle, and the Marqués didn't choose to enlighten him. At that point in the game a pawn had only one purpose—to protect the vulnerable queen; the carpenter's dingy quarters could serve as a dependable refuge for the *Mona Lisa,* a "safe house" which, regardless of what happened, would free the others to carry out their scheme.

In mid-September of that year (after the Apollinaire fiasco) Valfierno had a final meeting with Perugia, and shortly afterward he left France for America. His parting words to the obedient Vincenzo (they would prove to be his first mistake) were, "For the present, be careful of everything you say and do; don't arouse suspicion. Wait for new instructions, which I'll send you in a short while."

Perugia had assumed that the *signore* would now sell the stolen painting or ransom it back to the French, and that soon there would be more money for all of them. So he dutifully followed the Marqués's orders, with one minor exception. Evidently Françoise Séguenot, the laundress, grew more and more nervous about having the incriminating portrait in her possession and wanted to be rid of it. Since Perugia hadn't yet been cleared by the police, the gang decided to move the painting to Vincent Lancelotti's place at 57 Rue Bichat, in the same neighborhood as Perugia's own rooming house.

After work the group met at the Rue St.-Merri, retrieved the panel in its white tunic and burned the tunic in Mme. Séguenot's coal stove. Casting about for something else to wrap their prize in, Vincent picked up a piece of red velvet which his mistress had just bought and planned to use for a new skirt. Over Françoise's loud objections, the painting was wrapped in this red cloth. That night under cover of darkness *La Joconde* was taken temporarily to the new hideout, and Perugia, who had grown quite possessive of the lady, was gratified to have her so accessible.

Vincent and Michele Lancelotti both lived in the same ancient, run-down building on the Rue Bichat, the brothers having come originally from the village of Cernobbio on Lake Como, not far from Perugia's home in Dumenza. Throughout those critical weeks in Paris, Perugia often visited Vincent Lancelotti. He would glance into the cluttered cupboard for a glimpse of his precious velvet-wrapped panel; then, reassured, he would sit down to play his mandolin, drink too much *vino rosso* and reminisce with his homesick friends about their lives and loves in Italy. Joined in sad felicity, the expatriates would sing,

> *"Io te voglio bene assaie,*
> *E tu non pienze a me..."*

> I yearn for you very much,
> And you don't think of me ...

All that time the carpenter waited for the police interview which the *signore* had warned him about. Fortunately his stolid nature—not to mention dreams of future opulence—sustained him during this particularly tense period. The ponderous administrative wheels of the Paris Prefecture turned very slowly, and it wasn't until late November, three full months after the theft, that the knock came which Perugia had been expecting.

When he opened his door he saw a burly man in a dark coat and derby hat, and with him was a gendarme in uniform. The man, Inspector Brunet of Lepine's department, produced his credentials and stated that they had orders to interview Perugia and search his rooms. The carpenter invited them inside, offered Brunet the better of his two rickety chairs, and while the gendarme poked under the bed and peered diligently into bureau drawers the examination got under way.

Again, the innate cunning and ingenuousness of this simple-minded Italian workman cannot be overemphasized. Perugia, when he chose, could be lively and amusing; he was also a gifted actor with the survival instincts of a cornered animal. The record indicates that at this vulnerable moment he completely disarmed the veteran Brunet (as he would do to others later) and, fresh from the most audacious crime in the history of the Louvre, dissembled so successfully that he was given full clearance.

The official transcript of this interview reads in part:

Report of Inspector Brunet,
26 November 1911—

. . . The man Perugia, Vincent-Pierre, born 8 October 1881 in Dumenza (Italy), has been living alone for the past year at 5 Rue de l'Hôpital-St.-Louis at a rent of 180 francs per year. Nothing unusual can be deduced from his manner of life during recent months. . . . From 25 July to 21 October of this year, he worked as a painter and glazier for M. Perrotti, a contractor located at 13 Rue de Maubeuge. According to information received it appears that on 21 August last, Perugia, who is normally at work at 7 A.M., didn't arrive until 9 A.M., but we have no explanation for these two hours of absence. However, it often happens on Monday mornings that workers do not start their jobs on time. . . . During the questioning, he (Perugia) declared:

"I worked several different times at the Musée du Louvre while employed by M. Corbier, but especially on two occasions when we had to put glass coverings on some of the paintings. These were brought by the guards to rooms assigned for this work. They were then returned by the guards to their original places.

"I remember that the paintings from the Salon Carré were put under glass during the first session; at that time we were using for our workshop the Gallery of Italian Primitives. In order to get to our shop we had to use the staircase which is in the courtyard of the Louvre, under the clock.

"I had no idea where the *Mona Lisa* was hanging, and learned of its theft from the newspapers. I know nothing else about it."

Asked to explain the odd work gap on the very morning of the theft, Perugia shrugged. "I don't remember if I came two hours late to work on Monday, August 21; however, it's possible, and I suppose I must have fallen asleep again, which happens sometimes on Mondays."

His manner was so guileless, his smile so engaging, that Brunet apparently accepted all this, although given the circumstances—Perugia's work on the glass shadow boxes, his familiarity with the museum, his resemblance to the "man in the straw hat" described in the police fliers —it is puzzling that the inspector didn't pursue the matter more thoroughly. His report went on:

> ... Perugia worked for M. Corbier from 11 December, 1908, to 22 July, 1911. There were no complaints against him, and he left a rather favorable impression.

Brunet then summarized his examination, as well as interviews with several other men who had also worked on the Louvre's projects:

> ... In conclusion, the thorough investigations conducted in reference to the individuals mentioned in this report have produced negative results. No significant information was obtained to indicate that any of the workers in question participated in any way in the theft of *La Joconde*.

Perugia, incredibly, now had a clean bill of health from the authorities and his ordeal was over. He waited a respectable few days; then, with his friends' help, the *Mona Lisa* in her velvet finery was moved to her final hideaway. The carpenter lived in a combination bed-sitting room with a few old cupboards and a window opening on an air-shaft. There was also a tiny closetlike room under the eaves where Perugia stored tools, brushes, and some pieces of broken furniture which he planned eventually to mend.

His problem now was where and how to cache the painting. A false wall in the little storeroom was one possibility, but that would be risky: what if there was a fire and he had to get at the panel quickly? Fitting it into the back of one of the cupboards also had drawbacks; it would be a clumsy hiding place with no mobility. Finally Perugia decided to build a small trunk with a false bottom—a wooden box painted white, with brass reinforced corners and a leather handle on each end. That way the painting would be well hidden, yet could be easily moved without drawing any special attention to it.

With Vincent Lancelotti's help, the carpenter put the trunk together quickly; the *Mona Lisa,* still wrapped, was placed inside and a false bottom was fitted over it. Perugia threw in a few odd tools and pieces of clothing, for added camouflage. Then the trunk with its secret treasure was placed in Perugia's storeroom, and, pleased with this arrangement, the carpenter was at last able to relax. *Va bene, La Gioconda* was secure. All he had to do now was wait for orders from the *signore.*

PART FOUR

The Rift

One can certainly lose one's heart to a painting. I know a man who fell in love with the Mona Lisa. He is the one who had it stolen.

—GABRIELE D'ANNUNZIO,
interview in the
Tribune de Genève

19

THE PARIS YEAR dragged to a cold, soggy finale. Aged King Peter of Serbia came for a state visit and duly departed. The French Senate wrangled over a treaty with Germany aimed at settling the crisis in Morocco. Georges Carpentier won his match with Harry Lewis to become national boxing champion. It rained heavily on Christmas Day. The holiday revue at the Folies-Bergère featured Mistinguett, Yvonne Printemps and a young newcomer, Maurice Chevalier.

As for the *Mona Lisa,* it was nowhere to be found. The Sûreté had mounted a worldwide search, but one by one all its clues and promising leads had melted away, and by the spring of 1912 most Parisians accepted the fact that their treasure was gone for good. *"Eh Bien—C'est Vrai,"* read one sad newspaper headline, and it did seem true that *La Joconde* would never be seen again. As if to accent this, the traditional mid-Lent parade included a float showing a giant mock-up of the *Mona Lisa* taking off in an airplane from the roof of a cardboard Louvre.

Sales of *Gioconda* postcards, souvenirs and song parodies gradually declined, but curious rumors continued to flourish and would go on doing so for years. Georges Michel, a writer for the publication *Gil Blas,* revived the story that the painting had never really been stolen—that it had been damaged by a Louvre photographer and hidden in fear of the consequences; but when questioned officially, Michel had to admit that his report was based on hearsay.

Other rumors and innuendos kept popping up in the
wide wake of the Louvre robbery, and one involved the
world's most powerful financier. J. Pierpont Morgan,
then in his seventies, had at various times been labeled
a genius and a mountebank, a man of "thundering authority" and a manipulator "without a trace of moral scruples."
The banker's incredible wealth stemmed from his brain-
child, U.S. Steel, as well as vast holdings in coal, railroads,
heavy machinery, ship lines and electric companies. In
the vaudeville houses of America they sang about "Morgan,
Morgan, the Great Financial Gorgon," and by the turn
of the century his firm was so powerful that it could—and
did—save New York City from imminent bankruptcy and
in 1907 brought a halt to the United States financial panic.
During World War I, Morgan and Company met the
Allies' needs by floating $1.5 billion in bonds, and after
the war it underwrote an even larger amount for European
reconstruction.

The Great Financial Gorgon was also one of the most
avid and knowledgeable art collectors in history, his mam-
moth appetites backed by a bottomless purse. Describing
Morgan's passion for collecting, art critic Aline Saarinen
notes that it embraced not only sculpture and paintings but
Byzantine enamels and ivories, German boxwood carvings
and silver-gilt work, Italian majolica, antique tapestries,
Renaissance crystal goblets, Oriental porcelains, illumi-
nated manuscripts, jeweled clocks, rare snuffboxes and exquisitely painted miniatures of the sixteenth to eighteenth
centuries. "All this," wrote Saarinen, "in numbers that
made other collections seem pigmy in size: almost all of
this of unsurpassed quality."

Ever since the *Mona Lisa* had vanished, one of the
persistent rumors (with overtones of Valfierno) was that it
had been snatched by a corrupt dealer for sale to a mysterious private collector. At various times this recipient
was purported to be a French nobleman obsessed with the

lady's smile, a wealthy South American art historian, a
millionaire Chicago meat packer and a titled Russian who
kept a fabulous secret art gallery in St. Petersburg. In view
of all this, it wasn't surprising that the world's greatest
financier would be linked with the world's greatest art
theft. According to gossip on the boulevards, *La Joconde*'s
abductors had approached agents of the tycoon in hopes
of selling the painting to the Morgan collection. And on
April 13, 1912, readers of *The New York Times* found a
story cabled from Europe:

MR. MORGAN ANNOYED

> A report from Florence noted that J. Pierpont
> Morgan is much annoyed over the unfounded reports
> communicated to him today, that anyone had offered
> to sell him the "Mona Lisa."
> He declared that nothing of the kind had hap-
> pened and that nobody had offered him anything. He
> resented even that it should be imagined that he
> would have any relations with persons offering to sell
> stolen goods.

The item added that the banker "only wanted to be left in
peace like other citizens, to enjoy his vacation in Italy."

Despite his protests the elderly financier wasn't averse
to a little double-dealing of his own, spiriting "protected"
works of art out of European countries or skirting U.S.
customs laws when declaring values on his imported
treasures. But in the case of *La Joconde* his indignation
appears justified; such arrangements simply weren't the
great man's style, and he was too prominent and powerful
to be caught up in the blatant crime. Yet the story persisted,
and later his name would again be linked publicly to the
stolen portrait.

Meanwhile the last bit of optimism faded. During
most of 1912, hoping against hope, the Louvre's directors
had kept *Gioconda*'s place vacant on the wall of the Carré.

But by the end of that year they gave up and filled the spot with Raphael's portrait of the Renaissance courtier Baldassare Castiglione. It was a painful decision, signaling to the world that France no longer expected to recover her errant daughter; and art critic Robert de la Sizeranne wrote:

> One feels a certain malaise on seeing in the middle of the Salon Carré in the place of the familiar smile—the most feminine of all smiles—this man with his ample beard, with his skull tightly wrapped and haloed by an immense black biretta . . . who looks out at you calmly with his big blue eyes. One knew very well that the *Gioconda* would not be seen again, but it seemed that the place she had occupied for such a long time was a little hallowed, and that a man ought not to settle himself there in so comfortable and self-important a way.

Hallowed or not, the empty place was filled—Raphael had usurped his master, da Vinci—and France accepted the change philosophically.

Besides, there were other things to talk about. Another war had broken out in the Balkans. The popular Queen Wilhelmina of the Netherlands had arrived for a visit (dazzling Paris by dressing completely in white, from hats to shoes) and was soon followed by the exotic Bey of Tunis. In China, rebel armies toppled the Manchu dynasty. The world's newest and "safest" ocean liner, the *Titanic,* struck an iceberg and went down in the North Atlantic. The King of Sweden opened the fifth Olympic Games in Stockholm. England was paralyzed by a coal miners' strike; and Woodrow Wilson, Princeton scholar, was elected President of the United States.

There were still occasional postmortems on the whereabouts of *La Joconde,* but people thought about it less and less if they thought about it at all, and there seemed to be general agreement that the painting had been burned or damaged, hacked to splinters or secretly sold, lost at sea or hidden somewhere by a lunatic. *Par malheur,* it was gone forever and nothing more could be done.

Nobody knew, of course, that all this time the *Mona Lisa* was resting at the bottom of a trunk in a grimy closet in Paris, literally within walking distance of the great museum from which it had been taken. As for Vincenzo Perugia, the portrait's guardian, he waited with growing anxiety for instructions from his chief in America. Instructions which never came.

20

FOR CHARLATANS like Eduardo de Valfierno the times were made to order, fitting their needs and purposes as comfortably as their elegant custom-tailored suits.

Belle Époque, Gilded Age, Banquet Years—whatever the label, the era stretching from roughly the 1890s to the start of the First World War was unique in European and American history. It was not only a period of creative ferment but one of excess and contrasts: lavish wealth and frivolous waste living side by side with starvation, naïveté with cynicism, and dark forebodings with a jaunty optimism which would soon be shattered by two pistol shots at Sarajevo.

In the United States the mood was extravagant. Technology, that twentieth-century miracle, had brought the country electricity, motorcars, skyscrapers, aircraft, canned food, nickelodeon movies, the talking machine and 210,000 miles of railroads—with more wonders to come, including McKinley's vision of a "full dinner pail" for everyone. In view of all this, the paradoxes in booming America were perhaps more glaring than elsewhere. Those were years in which an antique faience soup bowl could bring $14,400

at auction, a sum equal to the combined annual wages of
thirty-five to forty female office workers in New York or
Chicago; years in which socialites could sail for European
holidays with as many as a dozen trunks, plus mounds of
chests and suitcases, while thousands in the slums went
threadbare.

The times were competitive, and if you had money
you spent it blatantly. William K. Vanderbilt's palace on
Long Island included a garage with room for one hundred
automobiles. Cornelius Billings, in the 1905 "season," gave
an equestrian dinner in Sherry's grand ballroom with
waiters dressed as grooms and all his guests mounted on
horseback throughout the meal. The O. H. P. Belmonts
were also horse fanciers. In the stables of their million-
dollar Newport "cottage," the thoroughbreds' stalls were
draped with pure linen sheets embroidered with the family
crest. It's conceivable that some of those sheets were manu-
factured by ten-year-olds, since at that time there were
almost two million child laborers between the ages of ten
and fifteen working a sixty- or seventy-hour week in the
country's coal mines, canneries, factories and cotton mills.

Valfierno the psychologist knew the operative rule: if
you were rich enough you consumed as conspicuously as
possible and tried hard to outdo your peers. Along New
York's Fifth Avenue, heading north from Forty-sixth Street,
tax-free wealth had built opulent marble neo-Renaissance
mansions and gaudy Italianate palazzos—a span of real
estate known as "two miles of millionaires." Similar epic
dwellings sprang up in other parts of the country; and all
these homes, with their myriad drawing rooms, dining
halls, libraries, bedchambers, galleries, ballrooms, lounges
and music salons, were soon crammed with elaborate
furnishings and works of art. In 1911—the same year that
the Marqués's agents snatched the *Mona Lisa*—a record
$17,330,000 worth of European art treasures were imported

into the U.S. These costly items (many fakes among them)
all but swamped the customs offices as the rich grabbed at
Old World culture and New World status.

Years earlier Valfierno had dipped profitably into this
great cornucopia, and now he returned for the biggest
coup. With his British and American colleagues, he quickly
set up headquarters in a fashionable New York hotel; here
the task force coordinated plans, collected their Chaudron
forgeries, then fanned out to make deliveries and complete
the secret transactions. The sale in Brazil was handled by
Valfierno himself.

With "infinite finesse," the Marqués later recalled,
the operators contacted their "nervously expectant buyers"
and delivered a superb Chaudron to each of them. First
came the guarded conversations, the ever-so-tactful references to the museum theft (still in the newspapers), the
discreet setting of times and places. Then a covert meeting
to hand over the carefully wrapped "da Vinci," the shock
of recognition and resulting excitement, finally the turning
over of substantial cash. The gang carried it all off with
aplomb: ". . . each buyer was certain that he possessed the
authentic *Mona Lisa,* and none would ever dare to solicit
an expert appraisal."

The plan had of course a fail-safe shield for the
swindlers: the moment the client took possession of his
"stolen" painting, he automatically became a co-conspira-
tor. If one of these men finally put certain facts together
and realized that he'd been cheated he would still be
trapped, since there was no way a victim could expose the
swindle without indicting himself as an accomplice.

But the Marqués had no cause for worry. It must be
repeated that he picked his marks with skill, choosing men
who trusted him implicitly and were delighted with their
"bargains." Seduced by Eduardo's flattery, impressed with
the robbery itself, deceived by the genius of Chaudron,

they had no reason at all to question the proceedings. Each felt deeply in Valfierno's debt; besides, it wasn't particularly unthinkable, in those free-wheeling days, to deal in illicit art. Nor is it today. As recently as 1972, the prominent California tycoon and art collector Norton Simon admitted candidly, "I spent between $15 million and $16 million over the last two years on Asian art, and most of it was smuggled." Simon was referring to various archaeological finds which had been slipped unlawfully out of their countries of origin, and his statements can be readily matched by collectors and curators everywhere.

The market for stolen art—substantial in Valfierno's time—has expanded vastly and is continuing to soar. Since the end of World War II, according to Interpol, over 40,000 works of art disappeared in Italy, more than 12,000 in France, and thefts are mounting in the United States, Belgium, Greece and Sweden. Many treasures are eventually retrieved, but scores of masterworks looted years ago from museums, churches, galleries and private homes haven't been seen again. There is, for instance, the classic Van Eyck panel, part of a large altarpiece, which was stolen in Ghent in 1934 and never recovered. It was later replaced by a copy. In Paris in 1959 a valuable Daumier painting was taken from a train, and hasn't been seen since. No fewer than twelve Old Masters were snatched from the Trèves Museum in southern France in 1968; all are still missing. That same year, Toulouse-Lautrec's *Marcelle* was stolen from a museum in Kyoto, and it is now on Interpol's "most wanted" list. In 1969 a Caravaggio was lifted in Palermo, and has never been traced; in 1970 it was a Correggio in Milan; in 1971 a Rubens and a Gauguin in Switzerland; and that same year a priceless Rembrandt disappeared from a private home in The Hague.

The list, of which this is a brief sampling, is a long

one and includes others such as Ingres, Monet, Picasso, Delacroix, El Greco, Hals, Vlaminck, Renoir and Utrillo. It can be assumed that these works (if not destroyed) are now somewhere in secret collections, enjoyed privately by their unlawful owners.

Valfierno's clients were men for whom acquiring a stolen masterpiece was an act of validation. For them, to possess was sufficient, even if the object had to be kept from most eyes. One psychologist, who chooses to remain anonymous, carries the syndrome further. "It isn't necessary," he observes, "for a compulsive owner to keep his prizes where he can personally enjoy them. They can be locked away in a safe, put in a bank vault, hidden in a warehouse. That's secondary—possession itself is all that matters."

In the world of art, the archetypal collector was undoubtedly William Randolph Hearst, the newspaper and magazine publisher whose acquisitive instincts were unrivaled even by Morgan. Hearst's obsession bordered on mania, and according to his biographer, W. A. Swanberg:

> It was understood everywhere that he could not take a normal view toward art, could not appraise a piece according to cold market value, set a top price and stick to it. . . . When he bid for something, it was seldom with a hard-headed take-it-or-leave-it attitude, but with the idea that he *must* have it. The thought of losing a piece to another bidder was sheer anguish. He was aware of his own weakness, but powerless to correct it.

During the 1920s and 1930s W. R. Hearst bought at a feverish pitch, and Swanberg notes that he was "a compulsive accumulator, fascinated by pictures in art catalogues, driven by an urge to buy and own things he might never set eyes on." In 1924 Hearst himself commented wryly, "I'm afraid I'm like a dipsomaniac with a bottle.

They keep sending me these art catalogues and I can't resist them."

The publisher's sprawling collections, ranging in quality from the superb to the shoddy, cost him well over $50 million. These artifacts not only overflowed his fabled palace, San Simeon, in California but filled 28,000 crates stored in two large warehouses on Southern Boulevard in the Bronx. A crew of thirty staffed the warehouses, including a dozen clerks who catalogued and photographed each incoming piece, two cabinetmakers who did nothing but maintain the antiques, and an armorer who cared for the vast collection of armor and medieval weapons.

Hearst, personally very honest, was taken advantage of by art dealers and usually paid highly inflated prices for everything. Curiously, Eduardo de Valfierno's friend and confidant Karl Decker was employed for many years by Hearst's newspaper empire. There is no specific evidence linking the flamboyant publisher with Valfierno's operations; but one can speculate as to the results if the most obsessive collector had ever crossed paths with the most gifted con man.

In recounting his story, the Marqués never disclosed the exact sums he received for the fake Leonardos; but according to other sources, each buyer handed over $300,000. With six forgeries to dispose of, this would bring the gang's windfall to $1.8 million—a substantial sum at a time when Macy's was advertising men's suits for $14.75, Bonwit Teller offered fur coats for $85, Axminster carpet went for $1 per yard, Saks and Company carried quality shirts at 90 cents each, a snappy Maxwell runabout could be had for $600, and eggs were 21 cents a dozen. Translated into today's dollar values, the scheme netted the ring the equivalent of $16 to $18 million.

When the cabal reassembled in New York City the

take was divided, with Valfierno retaining the lion's share. A number of minor figures who had been of help were also paid off. After finishing his work Yves Chaudron had remained in France, settling in a country house outside Paris; he had already received appreciable payments from the Marqués, and now an additional large bank draft was forwarded to him. For Chaudron it was not just a financial but a major creative triumph, and he reacted with "joy and pride when he learned the prices his work had brought."

As for Perugia and his two helpers, Valfierno claimed emphatically that they had received very generous payments at the time of the theft. According to the Marqués, "Perugia was paid handsomely—enough to take care of him for the rest of his days, if he had taken his good fortune with ordinary intelligence." The trouble was that Perugia didn't possess ordinary intelligence. Shrewdness and cunning, yes; but of basic intellect there was unfortunately little.

Now, with his forgeries delivered and the cash disbursed, the Marqués rewarded himself with a long period of gracious living in various exotic (nonextradictable) luxury spots in North Africa and the Middle East. But in the process, except for a few brief messages, Valfierno neglected Vincenzo Perugia. His first mistake had been to promise the anxious carpenter new instructions, which were never forthcoming. His second and more serious mistake was in failing to send additional cash, which would have kept his pawn solvent and quiet.

But the Marqués was now in the clear, and for the first time since the scheme was launched he grew complacent and careless. As a result Perugia became increasingly confused and began to feel that he had been unfairly abandoned.

21

ON THE BOULEVARD DE LA VILLETTE, in a bistro frequented by workmen like himself from northern Italy, Vincenzo Perugia drank *espresso* and brooded.

The *signore*—that faker, that *mascalzone*. How could a man so imposing, so distinguished, prove to be so false? After all the plans and arrangements, all the hard work and danger, nothing had come of anything. And now the man had disappeared into thin air. A few scribbled words from New York, Algiers, Port Said in Egypt (what was the *signore* doing in Port Said?), and after that—complete silence. As though he had ceased to exist.

The carpenter lit a black cigar and watched as it turned, like his hopes, into wisps of smoke. Perhaps it was to be expected. He never should have trusted that one; right from the start he had sensed something furtive, a certain slyness. Never again would he put his faith in criminals.

The money, like the *signore*, had also vanished. At first it had seemed a very great amount, but it had melted quickly. Ice in the hot Lombardian sun. He had been a fool to gamble over cards with the French—everyone knew they cheated. And the large sums he had bet on cycling and games of soccer—hundreds and hundreds of francs. What did he, a carpenter, know of teams and bicycles? He had spent a good deal on Mathilde, too, which had been unwise. Still, none of it would matter if the *signore* had done what he was supposed to do. If he had found a buyer for the painting, there would be riches enough for all of them. There *had* to be more money—Perugia had vowed years ago not to return to Dumenza until he had made his fortune.

Was it possible that the *capo* had died? Could that be

the simple explanation? Well, it no longer mattered—the man had never been very important. Wasn't he, Perugia, the one who had taken all the risks? Wasn't it he himself who had marched from the Louvre with Napoleon's loot, carrying it out right under their long French noses? Surely if anyone deserved rewards, *he* did. He was the real hero, not that other one with his elegant suits, lordly manners and deceptive ways. And, most important of all, it was Vincenzo Perugia who had *La Gioconda,* still hidden in her little wooden trunk. Not a soul in Paris knew about it except for Mathilde, the Lancelottis and that cow Séguenot.

Month after month he had followed orders, faithfully guarding the secret treasure, waiting in vain. But no more; the prize was all his, and now he would make plans of his own. . . .

For more than two years—from August 1911 to December 1913—the smile on the face of the *Mona Lisa* remained lost to public view. During that time, though their efforts gradually diminished, the masterpiece had been hunted not only by the French police but by Britain's Scotland Yard, the U.S. Secret Service and crack investigative units in Germany, Belgium, Greece, Austria, Spain and Czarist Russia. Despite this network of trained professionals, this great array of expertise, the search failed totally. And when the painting finally did appear it was without any help from the authorities.

Fragmentary records, letters, news items and statements by Perugia's friends and relatives make it possible to piece together a general picture of that two-year span; considering the stakes, a phase unique in the history of art heists.

Perugia's employment during those years was spotty. Though a skilled craftsman, he had trouble finding permanent work and wound up drifting from project to project with dry spells in between. From December 1908 to July 1911—during which time he helped build the Louvre's shadow boxes—he worked on and off for M. Corbier. Shortly after, he was hired by Perrotti and Company on the Rue de Maubeuge, and it was at this point that the actual robbery took place. In November he shifted to M. Ginoux, a painting contractor on the Rue de Trévise. He apparently stayed with Ginoux through most of 1912, after which he took on a succession of odd jobs and free-lance assignments. It was during this period, with his income cut to a trickle, that Perugia began dipping into the funds which the Marqués had given him.

Evidently the carpenter, like Apollinaire's friend Géry Pieret, was addicted to gambling. Valfierno theorized at one point that Perugia may have drifted down to the French Riviera and squandered his money there; but this is unlikely. In those days the pleasures of the roulette table and the racecourse—Longchamp, Chantilly, St.-Cloud, the steeplechases at Auteuil—were confined largely to the affluent; but the working classes had their equivalent diversions. Card games for high stakes could often be found in smoky back rooms of bistros near Les Halles, Parmentier and Goncourt. Rugby and soccer matches were played regularly in the Bois de Boulogne with team partisans eager to take wagers. There were also boxing matches, or *savates,* in which the contestants used their feet as well as their fists. And on Sundays a betting man could take in the popular bicycle races held in crowded *vélodromes* at Levallois, Vincennes and Charenton. Such temptations undoubtedly ate up Perugia's capital and hastened the crisis.

During this phase he was also involved in a romance with a young lady who has been identified only as "Mathilde." *Petit Parisien,* investigating the matter in December 1913, reported that Mlle. Mathilde worked as a cleaning woman in "a middle-class household," was attractive, had been born in Alsace and spoke French fluently but with a slight German accent. According to Perugia's neighbors, Mathilde and Vincenzo were quite smitten with each other; whenever she had a few hours to spare, the housekeeper would rush off to the Rue de l'Hôpital-St.-Louis to meet her lover. "She often," added the newspaper account, "came to the house where the *Mona Lisa* was hidden."

By the summer of 1913, Perugia had begun to tire of the romance, and neglected to answer the young lady's ardent letters. That October, after he failed to keep several dates with her, she hurried to Perugia's rooming house (she evidently had free access to his room), but he had managed to slip away earlier. The usual tears and entreaties got nowhere, and Mathilde finally accepted the inevitable. Very soon afterward she married an "honest, hard-working" young man who was en route to Nice to take a job as a house servant. Mathilde accompanied her new husband to the south of France—but her brief interlude with the guardian of the *Mona Lisa* would have repercussions.

Perugia, like other Italian craftsmen in Paris, felt rootless but was seldom alone. The district around the sprawling Hôpital-St.-Louis was a lively Italian enclave, and contingents from Turin, Brescia, Milan, Bologna and elsewhere all had their favorite cafés, restaurants and boarding houses. Not only did Vincenzo stay close to the Lancelottis, but numerous family members from the Lake Como area kept popping up in Paris, looking for work. Among them were his first cousins Giuseppe and Antonio Perugia, also two brothers named Moro. Another relative, Giovanni Perugia, arrived on his doorstep, and one Gaetano Girondi, a cousin through marriage, turned up and actually moved in with Vincenzo for several months.

Later, questioned at length, both Giovanni and Cousin Gaetano mentioned that they had seen Perugia's

wooden trunk in the little storeroom; in fact, while searching for pieces of lumber, Giovanni sometimes had to shove
the chest aside. Once he had lifted the lid and peeked in,
but, as he told the police, it contained nothing but "some
of Vincenzo's old clothes."

The carpenter's uncanny skill at play-acting and stay-
ing tight-lipped is again evident: neither of these two men,
living in cramped quarters on close terms with Vincenzo
Perugia, had any idea whatever that in the bottom of that
trunk was the most sought-after portrait in the world.

During those long months of waiting, a gradual psychological shift took place in the carpenter's thinking. The
Marqués at first had been a dominant, near-hypnotic figure
on whom Perugia willingly depended; but the swindler's
growing neglect was matched by Perugia's growing dis-
enchantment. For most of that first year Vincenzo clung to
hopes that the *signore* would pull off the sale of the century
and soon return to Paris, his pockets bulging with *denaro*.
It must be remembered that Perugia knew nothing of the
real scheme and the Chaudron forgeries; the Marqués had
indeed pulled off the sale of the century, six times over, but
as far as Perugia was concerned the *Mona Lisa* was still
in limbo, an untapped vein of gold, and nothing was being
done to exploit it.

Meanwhile, publicity about the great theft had
diminished and talk in the cafés of Paris centered not on
La Joconde but on Sarah Bernhardt's new film, *Camille*,
the drive to create a French air force of five thousand
planes, the latest anarchist disturbances, and an eclipse of
the sun, predicted for mid-April.

Perugia's funds at that point were almost gone, but
other forces were at work: his initial confusion had turned
to bitterness, then to anger, finally to a decision to defy the
signore. And, in his simple way, he began to think of himself as having acted *completely alone.*

Vincenzo had always been devoted to his father, who was a bricklayer, and to the rest of his family in Dumenza. Fourteen months after the robbery—in October 1912—he sent them a letter in which he wrote: "As for my behavior, you may say that it hasn't been that of a true son. But I beg you not to worry—in my own way of doing things lies my secret." He said in the same note that he expected to leave France soon and would do some traveling. He didn't explain why, but added, "I love you very much, and I hope to make your fortune." In closing he repeated, "Soon I shall make you all happy."

It seems evident that the single-minded carpenter was beginning to create a drama with himself as the sole player. This obsession grew, and by the summer of 1913 the *signore* had become a nonperson, almost erased from his thinking; even the faithful Lancelottis were brushed aside in Perugia's need to see himself as a lone hero, guided, incidentally, by the highest and most patriotic of motives.

As for the Marqués, he knew nothing of all this until much later. In fact, as he traveled about enjoying the fruits of his triumph, he had temporarily lost interest in the stolen painting and its guardian who he assumed, mistakenly, would remain obedient.

Valfierno said later that he had always intended, at some future date, to return the real *Mona Lisa* anonymously to the Louvre. Such a step could have effectively undercut the Sûreté and brought the entire episode more or less safely to an end: the museum curators would, after all, have their masterpiece back, the ring would have its profits, and the victims would have their "prizes." Comforting these not-so-innocents, if necessary, would have been child's play for Eduardo.

"But of course," he would reassure them as he had done many others, "the French have been so terribly embarrassed, so humiliated. *Évidemment* they had no choice;

they had to put in a substitute. But their painting is a forgery. All you have to do is compare the two, and you can see it immediately."

The Marqués would probably have been successful in thus bringing the scenario to a tidy end. But Perugia had ideas of his own for the *Mona Lisa,* and as 1913 drew to a close he was ready for the final gamble.

PART FIVE

The Recovery

> *The air redounds with a single senti-*
> *ment, an old saying that holds all the simple*
> *poetry of the Tuscan soul: "It seems like a*
> *dream!"*
>
> —*News item in* La Nazione

22

THE CITY OF FLORENCE on December 10, 1913, was bleak and cold, and in the Stazione Centrale the plumes of smoke rising from the locomotives seemed coated with frost. The early train from Paris via Dijon, Lyons, Mont Cenis and Turin had just arrived and its passengers climbed down from it wearily. Among them was a stocky young man in a rumpled overcoat, carrying a wooden chest which had once been painted white but was now scuffed and dirty.

Perugia, tired after his long journey, hoisted the trunk to his shoulder, crossed the piazza and walked past the Church of Santa Maria Novella. At the intersection he looked south to catch a glimpse of the Arno, and beyond it the familiar Tuscan hills with here and there a buff-colored villa set off dramatically by cypresses, parasol pines, and olive groves of silvery green. The carpenter pulled up his coat collar against the cold, smiled at the welcome sight and headed toward the nearby Via Panzani.

On that street, not far from Il Duomo, the great cathedral topped by Brunelleschi's mighty dome and flanked by Giotto's bell tower, was a small run-down hostelry called the Tripoli-Italia. The hotel's bored *portinaio,* dozing behind his desk, looked up as a stranger came through the door into the seedy stamp-sized vestibule. He asked for the cheapest room available; the clerk nodded, reached for a brass key and pushed the register along the counter. Perugia signed the dogeared page slowly, took his key, hefted the trunk and trudged upstairs to Room 20 on the third floor. Indifferently the *portinaio* glanced at the book; the new name in the register was "Vincenzo Leonard."

In his shabby room Perugia shoved the trunk under the high bed, pulled off his shoes and leaned back on the bedcovers. A long tiring journey, but a successful one. Yes, everything had gone well, especially when the train went through the Mont Cenis tunnel and stopped at the Italian border. He had stayed alert, and when the customs guards came into the crowded car he had opened the trunk without waiting to be asked. It was *disarmo*—the perfect innocent gesture—and the guards had barely looked inside. Besides, they were quite used to migrant Italian workers traveling at certain seasons between the two countries—that is, when they could afford the fare.

Perugia reached into his pocket; he had only a handful of francs left, so the trip had come none too soon. But now at last he and the madonna were safe in Italy. He would rest for a little while, have a bowl of soup, then pay a call on Signore Geri.

Alfredo Geri, plump, jovial proprietor of the Galleria Borgognissanti, was one of the busiest and best-known antiques dealers in Florence. His own involvement in this story began in November 1913, when he received a crudely written letter from Paris. The letter writer described himself as an Italian citizen who had been "suddenly seized with the desire to return to his country at least one of the many treasures which, especially in the Napoleonic era, had been stolen from Italy." The writer then confided that he had the *Mona Lisa* in his secret possession; he wasn't asking any specific price, but added that he was poor and needy. The note, signed "Leonard," gave his return address: a postal box on Paris's Place de la République.

Geri was of course inclined to throw the letter into his wastebasket as the work of a crank or silly hoaxer; but the more he thought about it, the more uncertain he became. *La Gioconda* had been missing for over two years, no clues had turned up, and the search had long since come to a dead end. Wasn't it vaguely possible that the portrait really *was* in the hands of this mysterious Leonard? Could Geri afford to ignore so provocative a lead?

The next day, the troubled dealer showed the letter to his friend Giovanni Poggi, director of Florence's prestigious Uffizi Gallery. Originating with the art collections of the Medicis, the Uffizi had become one of the world's great repositories of Old Masters; among its myriad paintings were Botticelli's *Birth of Venus,* da Vinci's *Adoration of the Magi* and priceless works by Michelangelo, Titian, Raphael, Fra Filippo Lippi, Giorgione, Tintoretto, Piero di Cosimo and Paolo Veronese. Poggi, as director of this vast collection, naturally enjoyed the highest standing in the Florentine art world, and his opinions mattered.

The *direttore,* after reading the message, shared his friend's skepticism, but felt that they had to follow up the clue no matter how preposterous it might seem. Geri was to write and express an interest but tell Leonard that naturally he would have to inspect the portrait before he could decide anything. Meanwhile, Geri and Poggi agreed to keep the matter quiet between them.

A flurry of letters and telegrams now ensued, with Leonard/Perugia suggesting various dates and meeting places, but nervously changing his mind. Then on December 9 Geri received a wire, routed through Milan, that Leonard would definitely be in Florence the next day and would come to the Via Borgognissanti. At that time Professor Poggi was in Bologna at the Severi, and Geri telegraphed him immediately if slightly inaccurately: "OUR PARTY COMING FROM MILAN WILL BE HERE WITH OBJECT TOMORROW. NEED YOU HERE. PLEASE RESPOND. GERI."

Poggi replied instantly by wireless that he would wind up his business and hurry back to Florence and could be at Geri's gallery on Thursday afternoon.

In the confusion and excitement of subsequent events,

there are the usual conflicting versions of exactly what took place and when, and intriguing contradictions have emerged which involve not only Perugia but Geri, Poggi and other officials. But it is now possible to present a picture of how the *Mona Lisa* reentered the world after her long hibernation.

Perugia went to the gallery that Wednesday afternoon and had his first meeting with Alfredo Geri, who talked to him in his study after curtaining the windows and securing the door. According to *La Nazione*, Florence's leading newspaper, the art dealer, after brief introductions, asked brusquely:

> "The painting?"
> "I have it with me," said Leonard, "at the boarding house."
> "It *is* the original?"
> "I guarantee it."
> "The original of this photograph?" insisted Signore Geri, showing him an excellent picture of the *Mona Lisa*.

Perugia studied the photograph for a long while, then replied carefully, *"I repeat: we are dealing with the real Gioconda. I have good reason to be sure."*

At that point, with a need to justify his statement, Perugia sketched the whole story of the theft for the surprised dealer—but he edited it to make it seem that he had managed the whole thing alone. Still probing, Geri asked, "How did you know my name? How is it you picked me from among all the antique dealers in Florence?" Vincenzo answered, "I read your advertisement in the *Corriere della Sera*." The dealer nodded; he had recently placed ads in a number of Italian, French and German newspapers, stating that he was "a buyer at good prices of art objects of every sort." Next Geri brought up a touchy subject, his version

of which was indignantly denied by Perugia. It had to do
with payment:

> GERI: What did you have in mind?
> PERUGIA: Five hundred thousand lire.
> GERI: That's fine, That's not too high . . .

The sum mentioned was the equivalent of about
$100,000; but just who initiated the subject of money was
to become a major dispute between the two men. Geri then
asked if Leonard had had any accomplices in the scheme.
Perugia "was not too clear on that point. He seemed to
say yes, but didn't quite do so. Yet he gave him to understand more 'yes' than 'no.' "

At this point Geri and his visitor parted company,
agreeing to meet the next day at 3 P.M. in the same office.
The dealer explained casually that Professor Poggi of the
Uffizi would also be there, and that all three could then go
to the hotel to examine the painting.

Leaving Geri's office, Perugia turned and headed
toward the embankment of the river; he was fatigued by
the events of the day and needed some quiet moments to
think. The carpenter walked along the Lungarno Corsini
and crossed the honey-colored Ponte Vecchio, the ancient
bridge dating back to Roman times, with its numerous tiny
shops clinging precariously to its flanks. On the far side he
found a cheap restaurant and had something to eat. Then
he headed back to his tiny room on the Via Panzani, fell
into bed at last and went promptly to sleep.

The next afternoon, shortly after three o'clock, the
group met as planned at Geri's office. Giovanni Poggi,
elegant and cultivated (did he remind Perugia perhaps of
his former mentor?), was already there, and Geri introduced them. In the presence of persons of rank, Vincenzo
tended to lapse into a rather pompous form of speech and
behavior; and now he seized the *direttore*'s hand enthus-

iastically and announced "how glad he was to be able to shake the hand of the man to whom was entrusted the artistic patrimony of Florence." The men soon left for Perugia's hotel. Geri, in a later interview, recalled:

> Poggi and I were nervous and anxious, but Leonard, by contrast, seemed quite calm. We arrived in the little room that he occupied on the third floor of the Hotel Tripoli-Italia. He locked the door, then drew out from under his bed a trunk of white wood that was full of wretched objects: old clothes, broken shoes, a mangled hat, plastering tools, some paint brushes, even a mandolin. He dumped all this on the floor in the middle of the room. Then, from under a false bottom in the chest, he took out an object wrapped in red cloth. We placed it on the bed and to our astonished eyes the divine *Gioconda* appeared, intact and wonderfully preserved. We took it to the window to compare it with a photograph we had brought with us. Poggi examined it and there was no doubt that the painting was authentic.

Geri and his associate were dumbfounded—and deeply moved—at this fantastic turn of events which had suddenly brought *La Gioconda* into the open. As for Perugia, he remained cool and detached, staring at the portrait and "smiling complacently, as if he had painted it himself." Next Poggi advised the workman—still known to them as "Leonard"—that he would have to take the portrait to his own office for safekeeping and for further tests to verify its authenticity. He assured Perugia that if all turned out properly, "your fortune is made." Vincenzo readily agreed. He rewrapped the painting in its red velvet, and all three took it by coach to the Palazzo degli Uffizi, the huge sixteenth-century edifice which housed not only the famous Picture Gallery but at that time the National Library and the Central Archives of Tuscany.

After locking the office doors Poggi and Geri, greatly

excited, began to check the panel in detail, comparing it with various closeup photos which had been made earlier at the Louvre. Everything seemed to conform—the same vertical crack in the upper left area, the same fading in the pale cerulean hills of the background, the same *craquelure* patterns on the lady's face and hands. Certain markings on the back of the panel also matched those previously recorded. Their last doubts disappeared; it was indeed the long-lost da Vinci.

Perugia had been waiting patiently through all this and now had to be dealt with. Playing for time, Professor Poggi told him that it was best not to rush matters; before anything could be settled, they would have to get "instructions from Rome." Vincenzo, a bit disappointed, asked them to hurry things along—he was, after all, short of funds and it was very expensive for him to stay in Florence. The others gave him their assurances, shook his hand warmly and thanked him again for making so patriotic a gesture. With that Vincenzo left the Uffizi and headed back to the Tripoli-Italia; but as soon as he was gone Poggi reached for the telephone.

Several hours later, answering a knock on his door, the carpenter found the chief of police of Florence, Francesco Tarantelli, standing there, flanked by two of his burly *poliziotti*. A surprised Perugia was then placed under arrest for the theft of the *Mona Lisa* and summarily whisked off to the local lockup known as Murate prison.

The next day, December 12, was one of frenzied activity at the Uffizi Gallery as word leaked out that the *Gioconda* had miraculously returned. Corrado Ricci, noted scholar and director of Italy's Department of Fine Arts, the "Belle Arti," rushed to Florence from Rome to take personal charge. Other art experts were deputized to meet at the Uffizi, examine the panel once more and decide on

its validity. While the portrait's unhappy kidnapper languished in his jail cell, this committee conferred and
agreed with Poggi's opinion: the painting, they said, was
authentic.

Corrado Ricci immediately telephoned Signore
Credaro, the Minister of Public Instruction in Rome,
with the good news. He in turn notified an aide of King
Victor Emmanuel III, also the French ambassador to Italy
and the Papal Secretary of State, who hurried to inform
Pope Pius X. In an imposing building near the Piazza
Colonna, the Chamber of Deputies was conducting business as usual—that is, a hectic fist fight was under way as
extremist delegates tried to block a vote on electing a
national deputy for Rome. The Information Minister suddenly rushed into the fray waving a telegram from
Florence announcing the story, which he read in a loud
voice; and the angry free-for-all ended in a flurry of shouts,
cheers and amicable embraces.

Now it was time for the incredible story to be
released: *La Gioconda* had been recovered! When big
headlines appeared on the following day and the surprising
details began to unfold, readers all over the world were
electrified. But none, perhaps, followed these events with
more attention than a select group of art connoisseurs
across the Atlantic—five in the United States, and a sixth
in South America. The news also bemused a certain
Argentine gentleman who had been taking his ease in
Morocco.

23

THERE WERE front-page stories everywhere, and readers
devoured the still sketchy facts in Rome and London, in

Oslo, Vienna and Antwerp, in Berlin, Budapest, Moscow and Madrid. On December 13, 1913, a page-one *New York Times* report was headlined:

FIND "MONA LISA"—
ARREST ROBBER

*Picture Recovered in Florence
Officially Identified as
Da Vinci Masterpiece*

REVENGE IS THIEF'S PLEA

The paper carried several columns on the background and known details of the theft, and added that Théophile Homolle, though long since dismissed from his post at the Louvre, was "overcome with joy when he learned of the recovery."

That joy—with a few exceptions—was universal, and congratulatory messages flooded into the Uffizi and the Belle Arti from all over the world. The Minister of Public Instruction soon announced that *La Gioconda* would be sent back to France, "with a solemnity worthy of Leonardo da Vinci and a spirit of happiness worthy of the *Mona Lisa*'s smile." He went on to say that, although the masterpiece was "dear to all Italians as one of the best productions of the genius of their race," it would be gladly returned to its foster country "as a pledge of friendship and brotherhood between the two nations." The Italian government asked France's permission to exhibit the painting in Italy before its return, and the French agreed with deep expressions of warmth and gratitude. The *Mona Lisa,* in fact, seems in a subtle way to have strengthened the bonds between these often contentious countries, and goodwill flowed on all sides. M. Kochlin, president of Les Amis du Louvre, announced that the person responsible for rescuing the painting (presumably Alfredo Geri) could now claim the reward of 25,000 francs; and President Raymond Poincaré's government was said to be planning "high honors" for all those who played a part in *La Joconde*'s recovery

As for Perugia the culprit, he was furious at being jailed and within hours had begun to talk freely. He confessed his identity to the police, told of his life in Paris and revealed facts about the 1911 robbery; but he distorted many elements of the story and was careful to keep himself squarely in the limelight.

In an account headed "PERUGIA IN THE MURATE," *La Nazione* stated that the prisoner was calm "but frequently expressed ill humor" at being behind bars. The reporter (adding his own flourishes) quoted an indignant Vincenzo:

> "I have rendered outstanding service to Italy," he said more than once. "I have given the country back a treasure of inestimable worth, and instead of being thankful, they throw me in jail. It's the height of ingratitude. . . .
> "See how ungrateful the Italians are," he kept saying. "If I had given the French authorities the means of getting the painting back, they would have given me at least a million. . . . But as a good patriot I have kept it hidden for two long years, and evaded every search, to bring it home to Italy—content to have half of what they would have given me in France!"

The journalist, confused but sympathetic, ended plaintively, "There must be some mistake which only the judicial authorities, the government, and above all public opinion, will soon clear up."

In France, excitement ran high but was tempered with caution; since the theft there had been numerous wild-goose chases and false alarms, and now many people were suspicious. On December 13 *Le Temps* reported:

Without calling into question the authenticity of the "Mona Lisa" returned to Florence, the curators of the Louvre are maintaining a properly discreet silence, and wish to say nothing until they have seen the painting. Certain descriptions of details and features give rise to some doubts among them. But they believe that these are probably due to errors in transmission, and that the painting will prove authentic.

The article said that identification would be made through full-sized photographs of the original, plus a special checklist of details:

Leprieur, curator of paintings, had compiled a number of observations on the portrait when it was reframed. These notes were then deposited with a notary in a sealed envelope. Obviously the curator's office in the Louvre wanted to take every precaution to prevent these characteristics and details from being used to help a forger . . .

The same thread of suspicion ran like a subtle motif through the arabesques of public joy and celebration. *Was this the real da Vinci? Could there have been a substitution during its years in limbo? Were the experts correct in their opinions?* A reporter in Florence wrote, "The recovery of *La Gioconda* continues to be a favorite topic of conversation in the political corridors," and went on to say, "At Montecitorio, the land of skeptics par excellence, it was natural for doubts to arise about the authenticity of Leonardo's painting. Even today quite a few people seem to doubt that the portrait recovered in Florence is the original."

Another news story reported: "Last year, an English gentleman went to his embassy in Paris saying that he had found the valuable painting. It was indeed the *Mona Lisa,*

but it was a poor modern copy and the impractical buyer
had been duped."

At the Uffizi, however, there was no hesitation. The
committee convened by Poggi to authenticate the portrait
included not only his staff but luminaries such as Commendatore Ricci; Count Carlo Gamba; Professor Luigi
Cavenaghi, curator of the Cenacolo in Milan, which housed
da Vinci's *Last Supper;* and Professor Luigi Grassi, a distinguished Florentine dealer with a gallery on the Via
Cavour.

Professor Grassi's grandson, Marco, now a prominent
art restorer with studios in New York, Florence and
Lugano, recalls a bit of family history: "When my grandfather died in 1937 I was only a baby, but my father often
spoke of the time when the *Mona Lisa* was brought to
the Uffizi. Grandfather was called late at night and had to
rush over to Poggi's office. It was all very secretive."

Marco Grassi is in his midforties, distinguished-
looking, with just a touch of gray at the temples. "Father,"
he adds, "was young then, but he remembered the excitement in Florence—the stories in the papers, descriptions
of the trunk, the crowds outside the little run-down hotel
on the Via Panzani."

Asked about the lingering doubts, Grassi shrugs. "My
grandfather was sure that the painting was genuine. But
he was terribly shocked by the whole episode; he felt it
gave the world of art a black eye. In those days in Italy the
major dealers were aristocrats, very highly respected. I
don't suppose he could even have understood this business
of treating art as a commodity—merchandise to be bought
and sold for speculation." The art restorer smiled. "The
professore was definitely of the old school. According to
Father, whenever the story of the theft came up he would
wince and change the subject. I think he took it as some
kind of personal insult."

Luigi Grassi's fellow citizens, without his scruples,

relished talking and reading about the new scandal; and in
England, France and Italy people were fascinated by
Perugia himself—this simple, uneducated near-peasant
who, in so offhand a way, had made monkeys of the
smartest, most powerful crime investigators in Europe. The
carpenter's exploits—as he described them—seemed almost
too bizarre to be true. *La Nazione* asked, "Did Perugia
have accomplices?" and in Paris, *Le Matin* hit close to
the mark: "He is a man with little education, an ordinary
worker. He has no technical knowledge and is ignorant of
things artistic. So it could not have been his idea to steal
the *Mona Lisa*. Perugia had to be acting on the instigation
of an outside party. . . ."

In Murate prison the celebrity was developing his own
scenario. His comments to the press grew elaborate and
contradictory, and reporters vied with each other to create
flowery phrases, presented them as verbatim quotes. One
interviewer had Perugia saying, "My work as a house
painter brought me into contact with many artists; I always
felt that deep in my soul I was one of them." Later, speaking of the stolen portrait: "I fell a victim to her smile and
feasted my eyes on my treasure every evening, discovering
each time new beauty and perversity in her." All along he
had claimed that his motives were patriotic, but now he
admitted that he also wanted "to insure a comfortable old
age for my parents." Why had he picked that particular
time to reveal his secret? Perugia's supposed answer marks
a new high in lyrico-poetic reporting: "I felt I must tear
myself away from the influence of that haunting smile. I
sometimes wondered in that two and a half years whether
or not I had not better burn the picture, fearing I should
go mad."

To clear up public confusion, it was announced that
there would be no extradition—the lady would return to
France, but not the carpenter. As an Italian national,
Perugia would be tried in Italy under Article 49 of the

46 HE RECOVERY

Penal Code. The French authorities fully concurred and
M. Viviani, Minister of Information, again offered cooperation and expressed "our gratitude to the Italian
government."

Like the *Gioconda,* Vincenzo Perugia had become hot
copy, and newsmen swooped down on the little village of
Dumenza to interview his confused family and friends.
They described the simple surroundings, talked to the town
mayor, Signore Corsini, and reported that the Perugias
were admired and respected locally. They also filed emotional accounts of Vincenzo's elderly father, the bricklayer,
who "seemed overcome" and refused to believe that his son
could be guilty of the theft: "Weeping, he said that his
son had always been kind and respectful to his elders, loved
art, and was good at playing the mandolin."

A more significant visitor to Dumenza was one
Lieutenant Barisone, an investigative officer of the *carabinieri.* Two workmen who had known Perugia in France
acknowledged to Barisone that they thought him somewhat
crazy, and added, "He worked hard, earned money, then
squandered it all." During this probe it also came out that
early in 1913 Perugia had made a sudden, unexpected trip
to London. The investigator learned that before leaving
for Dieppe and the Channel boat he told friends in Paris
that he would soon be back "with his pockets well lined,"
and it was now assumed that the London jaunt had been
for the purpose of selling the *Mona Lisa.*

The carpenter's "patriotism" soon received another
blow. In Paris, police searched the room where he had
lived and where *La Joconde* had been hidden; in addition
to some old clothes and a packet of love letters from the
elusive Mathilde, they also found a fragmentary diary. This
contained, in Perugia's scrawled handwriting, a list of art
dealers and wealthy collectors in Italy, Germany and the
United States. Among the American collectors purportedly
on the list were Andrew Carnegie, John D. Rockefeller

and J. P. Morgan. There were no references to Valfierno, the Lancelottis or any others involved in the robbery. This surprising find totally undercut Perugia's claim that he wasn't after money; whatever he was to say later—and to half-believe—it was clear that he saw the *Mona Lisa* as his one chance to get rich.

Curiously, the incriminating diary later disappeared from view; it cannot be found today in the files of the Paris Prefecture of Police, nor was it forwarded at that time to the public prosecutor in Florence. What's more, it was never introduced in evidence at Perugia's subsequent trial. Somewhere the document vanished and must remain an unresolved mystery, but it prompts certain questions. Was this potential evidence accidentally lost, carelessly overlooked or deliberately suppressed? And if the latter, for what reason?

Two weeks after that search, in a footnote to the diary story, Perugia made a further admission. On December 27 *The New York Times* reported:

TRIED TO SELL "MONA LISA"

*Thief Says He Offered It to
J. Pierpont Morgan's Agent*

Vincenzo Perugia, in whose possession the police of Florence recently found the famous painting, "Mona Lisa," which mysteriously disappeared three years ago [*sic*] from the Louvre, was examined today by the Magistrate who is investigating the case. The prisoner said he had tried to sell the "Mona Lisa" to a representative of the late J. Pierpont Morgan, and also had offered the portrait to various dealers in London, Paris and Naples.

Perugia's statements amazed the court because, assuming his confession to be true, it is remarkable that none of the dealers notified the police.

This was just one of the puzzles that now arose in the wake of the portrait's recovery. Vincenzo's comments added to the confusion; at that point his grip on reality was somewhat less than secure, making it difficult to sort out truth from fantasy. In the weeks to come he would make other admissions, but his mental state was such that at his trial he again completely reversed himself and posed as a selfless patriot. The matter was perhaps best summed up by an observer from *The Times* of London: "All's well that ends well, save for Vincenzo, who is still bewildered at finding his pains rewarded by prison and is convinced of an honorable release. What were really his motives, it would be hard to say. 'Mona Lisa,' who might tell, only wears her enigmatic smile."

Another participant in the scheme who might have told—but chose not to—had been wintering in Morocco when the startling news first broke. The Marqués de Valfierno was then in Casablanca, enjoying the climate and dabbling (to keep from getting rusty) in a vast real-estate boom that gripped the North African city, with worthless desert "property" selling for nine hundred francs per square yard.

In January 1914, some weeks after Perugia's arrest, Valfierno met his friend, Karl Decker, who was also traveling in Morocco on a newspaper assignment. Acting perhaps out of pique and vanity—plus a normal pride of craftsmanship—the aging con man decided to uncover the facts of this most remarkable of swindles. But first he swore his confidant to secrecy, which was to last for Valfierno's lifetime, and Decker scrupulously kept his part of this bargain for seventeen years.

The Marqués, Decker noted, believed that Perugia had taken leave of his senses by going to Italy, and was annoyed at the carpenter's defection which marred the classic symmetry of the original plan. However, he realized that recriminations were pointless. Valfierno had nothing personally to fear, since his tracks had been meticulously covered, and Perugia was obviously enjoying his solo performance, so the Marqués accepted these events more or less philosophically.

In a larger context, the master planner was satisfied: his scheme had been successful, and at that point he had no further interest in its repercussions. But while Valfierno's role in the drama was finished, there were other scenes waiting to be played.

24

PERUGIA, BASKING in all the attention, was merely a supporting player, and now the star moved from the wings to center stage. For the first few days the *Mona Lisa,* in an antique gilded frame, was displayed in a small salon at the Uffizi Gallery, protected by what seemed like a battalion of *carabinieri.* Here she held court for a privileged group of museum officials, art critics, administrators, government dignitaries and the inevitable reporters.

Once again the newsmen outdid themselves in conjuring up the gaudiest possible phrases for this historic occasion. Their joy and elation exceeded all bounds, and if there had been a special Aureate Prose Award it would surely have gone to Serse Alessandri, writing in *La Nazione*: "Around the painting . . . press the first fortunate few who timidly gaze and admire with little said, with none of the outbrusts of the enthusiastic chatterer: great joy cannot be translated by the facile turns of phrase of the habitual talker . . ." Alessandri saluted the men in charge of the recovered masterpiece,

> first and foremost Dr. Giovanni Poggi and Commendatore Corrado Ricci, who have spent days of feverish anxiety and vigil, in which the painting which smiles above all other smiles of art was, after centuries, to again receive here in Florence the ad-

miration of noted persons and the homage of Tuscan hearts. It has been a time of jubilant veneration, touched with melancholy because the painting will again leave Italy's shores . . .

Warming happily to his task, the reporter continued:

"Yet the sweet smile of *La Gioconda* tempted one to think that her inevitable departure might not be true; the divine creature seemed to have become sweeter than ever: she seemed to feel quite at home. The charming glint in her eye was reflected on every face; and everyone, lost in contemplation, remembered the poignant regret when they had admired her irresistible enchantment in the museum in Paris. The hearts of these admirers struck a supremely Italian chord. Said Nerino Ferri, a former director of our gallery, 'She came back for a breath of the air of home . . .' 'Yes,' murmured Adolfo Orvieto, erudite editor of *Marzocco,* in a low voice, after a keen searching look at her. 'She came back to us, but she's still living in Paris: that veil of morning mist which wreaths her dear face is because she does not have the supreme happiness of our Florentine sky.' "

Early on Sunday morning, December 14, the panel was shifted to a larger salon called the Self-Portrait Hall, and it was reported that the men who stood and watched slowly removed their hats as the painting went by. Here it was set on an easel flanked by portraits of Titian and Raphael, and the bottom of the easel was draped with the old piece of velvet. Then at 9:30 A.M. the doors of the Uffizi were opened so that *La Gioconda* could be viewed by the Florentine public.

Between 9:30 and 1 o'clock that afternoon an estimated thirty thousand people crowded, shoved, pushed and fought their way inside for a glimpse of Italy's most famous expatriate. They stood in long lines stretching through the Piazza della Signoria, stamping their feet and beating their arms to keep warm; then, once they were inside, their excitement reached near hysteria. Panes of glass were broken, several *carabinieri* were knocked to the ground, and a number of marble busts, endangered by the crush on the stair landings, were hastily evacuated. Guards struggled through the crowds cautioning everyone to remain cool and tranquil. *"Calmo! Sia fatta calmo!"* they pleaded. *"Tranquillo, per favore!"*

Despite all the crush and confusion the day was hugely satisfying, and in Rome the editors of *La Tribuna* wrote:

GIOCONDA ENTHUSIASM IN FLORENCE

Yes, everywhere it's the "Gioconda." Florence seems the apotheosis of beauty. No word is sought but "Gioconda." Nothing else takes place but talk of how long "Gioconda's" Italian journey will last and the pleasure of seeing it again. . . .

When the gallery closes, when twilight falls, we hope that . . . she will be placed in the window, in the corridor, so that she can watch dusk descend upon the Arno, a sunset she has never seen. She has slept for two years in the bottom of a trunk, wrapped up in a red cloth which is now folded around the easel. But if her sleep was disturbed, perhaps she would have happily accepted it if she had known that this was a prelude to such an exciting and triumphant return. . . .

For Professor Poggi the nervous strain proved a bit too much, and the article relates: "The other evening he was so emotionally upset that he had to go to bed."

After several days at the Uffizi, the star began her homeward journey—a trip, with its entourage of twenty, which all but matched the royal progresses of England's Queen Elizabeth in the sixteenth century.

Henri Marcel, new director of the Musée du Louvre, had already arrived in Florence to supervise the move; and on December 20 the *Mona Lisa* was placed in a beautiful rosewood case—far more appropriate than Perugia's crude trunk—and brought to Rome. In the Ministry of Fine Arts it was inspected by King Victor Emmanuel, his Cabinet ministers and members of Rome's diplomatic corps, then officially turned over by Minister Credaro to M. Barrère, the French ambassador. Next the portrait was put on display at the Borghese Gallery, the elegant villa rich in Italian history which had been built in the seventeenth century by Cardinal Scipione Borghese, who also founded the family's notable art collections.

Here the crowds outdid anything in Florence. Great throngs poured through the Porta del Popolo into the ornamental gardens, people crossed themselves fervently, women fainted in the crush, and extra squads of police were rushed to the scene. From its stay at the Borghese, the panel was taken to be exhibited briefly at the Villa Medici, then went to the Brera Museum in Milan; and everywhere the hectic scenes were repeated.

Finally the precious Leonardo, with its large escort of curators and protectors, was placed aboard the crack Milan–Paris express, and on December 31, 1913, Lisa del Giocondo ushered in the new year by crossing the French border amid widespread national rejoicing.

In Paris at the École des Beaux-Arts, officials of the Louvre were waiting with the envelope containing Leprieur's secret notes; behind locked door the painting was again inspected by experts, and within the hour came an official announcement that it was indeed genuine. All France welcomed the news happily, and a new *Gioconda* craze swept the capital. Parisian women bought special makeup so as to imitate *La Joconde*'s sallow complexion, café entertainers composed flowery new lyrics praising her, and souvenir vendors again did a lively business. A popular postcard, entitled "Her Return," showed the lady in the traditional pose cradling a baby in her arms, while behind her appeared the face of papa Vincenzo Perugia.

Another greeting card announced: "BEST WISHES FOR 1914 —LA JOCONDE WILL AGAIN BE RECEIVING, EVERY DAY EXCEPT MONDAY." And one poster carried its own verses:

> The *Mona Lisa* has been found
> After two long years of absence,
> She must have been around the world
> 'Ere ending up in Florence.
>
> What a time she must have had,
> Enough to go insane.
> But she has hurried back to us,
> For France she'll smile again.

For several days the masterpiece was on view at the Beaux-Arts and an admission fee was charged, the proceeds going to Italian charities. Then on January 4, 1914, in an emotion-filled ceremony, it was again placed on the Carré wall, exactly two years, four months and fourteen days from the morning Perugia and his helpers carried it away. The occasion was marked throughout the world, and an editorial in *The New York Times* noted: "Few Americans will omit from their itinerary next summer a visit to the Salon Carré."

Parisians were of course overjoyed, and *Le Matin* reported that in the next two days over 100,000 people came to the Louvre to welcome the painting home. One may speculate as to whether, in that incredible crowd, there might perhaps have been three unique visitors—specifically Mme. Séguenot and the Lancelotti brothers, who were about to reenter the story.

25

TEN DAYS after the *Mona Lisa* came to Florence—on the same day that the Italian government officially turned it over to the French ambassador—it was the subject of a lively confrontation at the Paris Prefecture of Police.

Months earlier, acting on a vague tip from Perugia's relative Gaetano Girondi, the gendarmes had collared Vincent Lancelotti and brought him before one of the judges investigating the case. Lancelotti had objected hotly, protested his innocence and denied any knowledge of the crime; and when a search of his room on the Rue Bichat yielded nothing (the panel was by then in the wooden trunk), the *juge d'instruction* was obliged to let him go. But on December 21, 1913, he, his brother Michele and his mistress Séguenot were again picked up—this time on the word of Perugia himself.

The next morning *Petit Parisien* headlined its story:

PERUGIA DENOUNCES HIS PARISIAN ACCOMPLICES, WHO ARE ARRESTED

They are the Lancelotti brothers and the mistress of one of them—Vincent, the principal suspect—was completely in the know about Perugia's projects, and hid "La Joconde" for two and a half months. . . .

In Florence, the unhappy carpenter had been subjected to a great deal of pressure, plus firm but subtle questioning. In a moment of weakness he broke down, began to weep and for the first time named his three associates. Soon he recovered his composure and, anxious to protect his role, retracted statements implying they had helped in the theft. After more questioning he would concede only that Vincent had hidden the painting for him and had helped build the trunk, and that both brothers had accompanied him to the Gare de l'Est when he began his trip to Italy.

Now, standing before Deputy Chief Niclausse at police headquarters on the Île de la Cité, the trio heard Perugia's accusations. Vincent immediately burst into loud denials, seconded somewhat feebly by his younger brother. According to the florid news accounts, Lancelotti shouted, "That's a lie! A whopping lie! I protest against this vile calumny—Perugia would never have said those disgusting things!"

There were more histrionics, then the workman calmed down a bit, looked around and announced, "Moreover, since you're accusing me, I'm going to get a lawyer and I will talk only when he is present, so you won't be able to distort what I say. I intend to leave here with my head held high!"

His performance was as nothing compared to that of Françoise Séguenot, whose melodramatics could have challenged Eleonora Duse and the Divine Sarah. Asked if she knew anything about the hidden painting, the rotund laundress offered a unique disclaimer: "I work at home as a washerwoman. Nothing, however small, could have been brought into our miserable little room without my noticing it immediately." As her discomfort grew under closer questioning, she cried, "What, me, a Frenchwoman, hide the *Mona Lisa*? If I had seen it in Perugia's possession, I would have torn it from his grasp and rushed it back to the Louvre!" Five minutes later, she passionately contradicted herself: "I have never seen the *Mona Lisa,* I swear to you! I can tell you, it was only when Perugia was arrested that I even learned that the painting *existed*. There's nothing surprising about that—I'm just a poor working woman and know nothing of art!"

For the calm, long-suffering deputy, this was a bit much. "You claim," he said, "that all the fuss about the theft at the Louvre didn't come to your attention? But, madame, that is childish!"

Séguenot stuck to her discredited guns, peppering her denials with outbursts against the hapless carpenter. "Perugia," she shrieked at one point, "is a pathetic creature, a coward! I'll strangle him with my own hands if I ever set eyes on him again. I always told Vincent that he would do him no good!"

She also explained why Vincent and Michele had gone with Perugia to the railway station: "When a compatriot is going home, the Italians usually go to the station to see him off. They ask him to do small services—see their friends or families. Really, what could be more natural?"

Late that afternoon, a somewhat groggy Niclausse reported all this to Judge Drioux, who read the transcripts and signed committal papers. Vincent Lancelotti was taken to La Santé prison; the others weren't jailed, but all three were charged with "complicity in larceny by receiving and concealing an art object stolen from a state museum."

None of them was ever brought to trial. The official *Gazette des Tribunaux* for April 26, 1914, noted: "M. Drioux, *juge d'instruction,* has just dismissed the indictment against the brothers Lancelotti and their [*sic*] mistress, who were charged as accomplices in the theft of the Joconde." The jurist had good reason for this. The trio had put up a strong united front, insisting on their complete innocence; the only evidence against them had been the shaky word of Perugia, who was six hundred miles away in Italy, and whose statements were growing erratic and unreliable. So there was simply no solid proof. A trial of this sort would also have meant added humiliation for the French; *La Joconde* was safe in the Louvre, the museum's security had been greatly improved, and to re-open the wounds on so vague a basis would have been politically unwise. Besides, the French soon had other problems involving their Leonardo.

In January 1914, Alfredo Geri collected his 25,000-franc reward and received the rosette of France's Légion d'Honneur, plus an honorary title: *officier de l'instruction publique.* But the picture dealer had more grandiose designs. Based on an unwritten Gallic tradition that the finder of a lost art object was entitled to a fee equal to ten

percent of the object's value, he sued the French government for ten percent of the value of the *Mona Lisa!*

This threw the Louvre curators and government
officials into a turmoil: not only did it entail paying a huge
sum of money, but how could the portrait even be evaluated? Who was qualified to judge its true worth?

Everyone was in a quandary. Durand-Ruel, dean of
Paris picture dealers, stated that at the very least he "would
ask half a million dollars if the picture were mine, with the
certainty that there would be so many offers that a much
higher price would be obtained." M. Schoeller, manager of
the well-known Georges Petit gallery, said, "The *Mona
Lisa* is certainly the most famous picture in the world, even
if not the greatest. I should class it in value with the
masterpieces of Velásquez and Rembrandt. My lowest
price would be over a million dollars."

According to *The New York Times,* most dealers and
experts refused to give a specific figure, claiming that *La
Joconde,* in view of its history, was priceless, and that there
were "probably several wealthy men, particularly in America, who would raise the bids to several million dollars if
the picture were placed on sale." All of which would have
been of interest to Valfierno's clients, who presumably
followed these events with mixed feelings.

After a lengthy battle in the French courts, Geri's
claim was turned down—partly, notes Roy McMullen,
"because he had allegedly done nothing but his duty and
partly, it seems, because no one knew how to calculate ten
percent of the inestimable."

Meanwhile, the kidnapper of *La Gioconda* remained
behind bars in Florence, but his imprisonment wasn't without its compensations. One part of the plan had in any
event been realized: Vincenzo Perugia had become a national celebrity. In Italy he was looked on with admira-
tion as a Quixote who had tilted at Gallic windmills, and
gifts for him began to pour in. There were flowers, bottles

of wine, jars of homemade soup, packages of food, cartons
of cigarettes. Female admirers wrote adoring letters and
sent pictures. People sent cash, one anonymous donor
contributing small sums which added up to over ten
thousand lire.

Though lonely and frustrated, Vincenzo enjoyed all
this attention and for a while remained cheerful. He read
a good deal and, thanks to the food packages, put on
weight; but as the weeks dragged by and his trial date was
postponed numerous times, he began to brood. Whenever
the subject of the *Mona Lisa* came up, he would grow
agitated and babble in a voluble but disconnected way.
Vincenzo's depressions increased and he had fits of weeping
which alternated with moments of euphoria. He was also
examined by a psychiatrist, one Professor Amaldi, who
came regularly to the Murate; at first Perugia was furious
at being questioned by an *alienista* and kept shouting, "I
am not crazy!," but he and Amaldi later became friends,
and the doctor gave helpful testimony at the carpenter's
trial.

During those months of waiting, Perugia protected his
image carefully. After his revealing statements about the
Lancelottis in December, he dropped that subject and
refused to speak of them again. Heroes are not, after all,
created by committees. Vincenzo was determined to play
out the role of lone patriot, and in that context accomplices were a drawback. To grasp his motives, it is necessary to realize the full range of his vanity and resentment
—all of which led, in his simplistic way, to a form of auto-
hypnotism and subversion of the truth. As Sigmund Freud
states, part of the infantile wish-fulfillment process involves
"the depreciation of reality—the neglect of the difference
between reality and fantasy."

Perugia's fantasy was bizarre but psychologically com-
prehensible. He *had* to reject Valfierno for inner reasons,
and after the arrest he became trapped in his delusions.

But he was still a gambler, and as his trial day drew near he kept hoping that somehow, miraculously, he would be vindicated.

26

IN THE SPRING of 1914, the twilight of peace and innocence in Europe, events large and small elbowed Perugia and the *Mona Lisa* from the front pages.

In Milan, parish priests launched an all-out war on the tango, warning their congregations not to indulge in this "immoral" dance, or even to watch it. In London, a hatchet-swinging feminist strode into the National Gallery and slashed Velásquez's *Venus with a Looking Glass*—in protest, she said, against the British government's imprisoning of the suffragette Sylvia Pankhurst.

In Mexico, revolution was raging; Pancho Villa's armies were on the march and President Wilson dispatched U.S. troops to briefly occupy Vera Cruz. In Germany, work was speeded on widening the strategic Kiel Canal to accommodate the Kaiser's giant new battleships. On April 21 England's King George V and Queen Mary came to Paris for a four-day visit, and *Le Matin* observed, "One has not seen such enthusiasm since the visit of the Tsar in 1896." Later that spring, the Louvre put on display its magnificent new collection of Impressionist art—a bequest of Isaac da Camondo which included works by Monet, Cézanne, Renoir, Sisley, Degas and Toulouse-Lautrec.

And on that same day—June 4, 1914—the former Louvre workman Vincenzo Perugia went on trial in Florence.

According to Italian law, even where there is a confession of guilt, a formal trial—really an extended hearing—must be held, and this then forms a basis for sentencing.

In Perugia's case the tribunal convened at 9 A.M. on the fourth and completed the taking of evidence in the course of that day. During the previous months Perugia had been questioned numerous times, and had made conflicting statements. At one point, for instance, he claimed that he took the painting on the spur of the moment, and that he picked *La Gioconda* by accident. Later he insisted that he had planned the theft for months and had chosen the da Vinci because he was obsessed with the lady's smile. At his trial, he came up with still a third version of this event. He also implied that he had hidden overnight in the museum—then changed his mind and stated that he had gone to the Louvre on Monday morning along with the maintenance men.

Vincenzo's vagaries and ambiguities are understandable, given his situation: his motive at that time was to suppress the fact (even from himself) that he had acted on orders from a higher-up, which led to much floundering and the concoction of assorted "plausible" explanations.

Presiding over this official tribunal was Cavaliere Barilli, assisted by two judges, Counselors Floriani and Susini. The public prosecutor was Cavaliere Bartoli, and the defendant was represented by two court appointed *avvocati,* Counselors Carena and Targetti.

The public is a wanton, and Vincenzo had gradually slipped from popular favor and attention. After a month or two the gifts and letters had faded away, and only a handful of spectators showed up for his trial, although these were augmented by a large number of court officials, guards, art experts, assorted witnesses, and reporters from Italy's major newspapers. The Italian authorities were not without sympathy for the young carpenter-painter who, whatever his motives, had carried the famous Leonardo safely to Florence and reaffirmed for the entire world the glories of the Italian Renaissance. There was no real desire to "punish" Perugia, nor to unravel all the tangles of the

Leonardo da Vinci's celebrated *Mona Lisa,* now on display in the Salle des États, Louvre, Paris.

A photolike painting by Louis Beroud, showing *La Joconde* in the Louvre, flanked by a Titian and a Correggio. This realistic view was painted sometime before August 1911, when the panel was stolen.

The Louvre's Porte Visconti. It was through this door, on a museum clean-up day, that the gang walked off with the *Mona Lisa* wrapped in a workman's tunic.

Below left, after the disappearance of the painting, Paris street vendors peddled song lyrics such as "Have You Seen Her—La Joconde?"

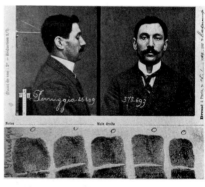

Official police photos of Vincenzo Perugia, after his earlier arrest in 1909. (Note misspelling of his name, also the fact that fingerprints show the right hand only.)

Pen sketch appearing in *Excelsior,* Paris, showing bare hooks on the wall of the Salon Carré after the theft. (Note bouquet of roses placed before the empty space.)

"La Joconde on a Spree," a ditty sung to the tune of "Auprès de Ma Blonde," enjoyed a lively sale in the weeks following the robbery.

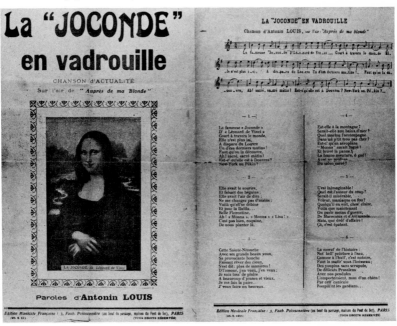

PHOTO ALINARI-VIOLLET

Perugia's shabby room in Paris, being searched by police after he was arrested in Florence. A revealing diary was found which later disappeared.

A poster typical of many which were circulated to celebrate *Lisa*'s return to France.

New Year's greeting card popular with Parisians in January 1914. The message notes: *"La Joconde* will be receiving again every day except Monday."

LE RETOUR DE LA JOCONDE

Elle est retrouvée la Joconde   Ce qu'elle a dû en faire un'bombe
Après 2 grandes années d'absence   Jusqu'à en tomber en démence
Elle a dû faire le tour du monde   Elle va nous revenir en trombe
Avant d'échouer à Florence   Elle va re sourire pour la France

souhait de bonheur
pour 1914

La Joconde
Reçoit de nouveau
tous les Jours sauf les
Lundi
musée du Louvre   Paris

The *Mona Lisa* reappears. Here, flanked by hand-picked *carabinieri*, it is on display in the Portrait Room of the Uffizi Gallery, Florence.

Collection of *Mona Lisa* counterfeits, assembled for the Paris Salon des Faux in 1955. Painting at the far right is believed to be an "original Chaudron."

PHOTO ALINARI-VIOLLET

An unknown Louvre copyist poses beside his painted version of *La Joconde*. (Photo dates from the early 1920s, during which period hundreds of copies of the portrait were made.)

Left, the "Isleworth version" — *Gioconda* owned by Henry F. Pulitzer, who insisted that this was the real *Mona Lisa* of da Vinci.

Opposite, the Vernon *Mona Lisa*—or "American *Joconde*" —claimed by the heirs of William Henry Vernon to be a genuine painting of Leonardo da Vinci's, a claim explored herein.

PULITZER PRESS

Raymond Hekking shown here with his *"Joconde* of Nice," which he claimed was painted by Leonardo. Seated at the desk is Milan art expert Professor Giorgio Nicodemi.

A two-page spread from the Time-Life World Library book *Italy,* published in 1961. The *Mona Lisa* caption refers to the Louvre's painting, but the photograph shows portrait owned by the Vernons.

Sketch by Raphael of Maddalena Doni, *circa* 1505, based on Leonardo's early *Lisa.* (Note the flanking columns.)

crime. In short, the trial was *pro forma;* yet in the interest of law and order—not to mention French amity—the judges were instructed to proceed as fairly and as diligently as possible.

The court records of Vincenzo's trial, plus certain news accounts, have managed to survive two world wars and the great Florence flood of 1966; and portions of that transcript are worth detailing:

President Barilli, after calling the court to order, asks the defendant to rise.

> PRESIDENT: What is your name?
> ACCUSED: Vincenzo Perugia.
> PRESIDENT: Your father?
> ACCUSED: Giacomo.
> PRESIDENT: And your mother?
> ACCUSED: Rosa Celeste.
> PRESIDENT: How old are you?
> ACCUSED: Thirty-two.
> PRESIDENT: Where were you born?
> ACCUSED: In Dumenza.
> PRESIDENT: Are you married?
> ACCUSED: No, sir.
> PRESIDENT: You are a house painter by trade?
> ACCUSED: I am *pittore.* [Perugia uses the word for "artist."]
> PRESIDENT: Have you ever been convicted of other crimes?
> ACCUSED: Well, yes . . . little things . . .
> PRESIDENT: I'll remind you of them. You were convicted twice—once for theft in Macon, and once for violent acts. All right?
> ACCUSED: Yes, but—
> PRESIDENT: You can give your justification later. Now you may sit down.

Perugia returns to his seat, and Cavaliere Barilli addresses the customary admonitions to witnesses and experts who will be called to testify. Targetti, speaking on behalf of the defendant, maintains that according to Article 5 of

the Penal Code the proceedings against Vincenzo Perugia
are illegal, since there has been no formal complaint by the
French government. Much buzzing in the courtroom. The
president reserves judgment on this matter. Vincenzo
comes forward again for questioning.

> PRESIDENT: Perugia, on the twenty-first of August,
> 1911, a painting by Leonardo da Vinci portraying
> the Gioconda was stolen from the Louvre Museum
> in Paris. You are the confessed perpetrator of that
> crime. Briefly relate what occurred.
> ACCUSED: Can I also tell why I decided to commit
> the crime?
> PRESIDENT: No. You will speak of the preceding cir-
> cumstances later. For now, limit yourself to recount-
> ing the details.

Perugia's brief account of the theft is inaccurate and
grossly oversimplified.

> ACCUSED: *Va bene.* At around six o'clock that morn-
> ing, I left home and went to the Louvre. I wandered
> through various rooms and finally reached the one
> where the portrait of the Gioconda was hanging. I
> thought the right moment for stealing the painting
> had arrived—so I took it and then cautiously left
> the museum.
> PRESIDENT: How did you leave the premises?
> ACCUSED: By the same door through which I entered.
> PRESIDENT: Your statement is in error.
> ACCUSED: *Perchè?*
> PRESIDENT: In order to leave, you had to remove
> several screws from a lock. Now, it is clear that if
> you had to do that to get out, you couldn't possibly
> have entered that way. . . . Didn't you yourself say
> you were almost caught by a workman, who came
> to open the very door on which you were trying to
> force the lock?

Perugia stammers vaguely, and *La Nazione* notes here:
"This circumstance of the door . . . is, and remains, some-

what confused. But the President expresses his opinion that it is not in fact of great importance, and moves on."

> PRESIDENT: Tell us about the paintings—those of great value at the Louvre. Are they fixed securely on the walls, or simply hung? In other words, is it easy to remove them?
> ACCUSED: It is extremely easy. They're only hung.

Perugia, at the president's request, presents the circumstances which led to the theft—the "strong patriotic impulse" which motivated him. As he develops this theme he assumes, according to *La Nazione*, "an attitude that is almost heroic."

> ACCUSED: I didn't study much in my early youth because conditions in my family didn't permit it. But through my reading, done here and there, I knew that almost the entire patrimony of France was once upon a time the patrimony of Italy. I thought about those robberies for a long time. Then, working in the Louvre, I learned more. I examined documents—
> PRESIDENT: Which documents?
> ACCUSED: Various ones. Many. I was in the library of the Louvre itself, and there were a lot of books and prints. I remember one—a picture of a cart pulled by two oxen; it was loaded with paintings, statues, other works of art. *Things that were leaving Italy and going to France!*

After a brief exchange in which Barilli attempts to calm the defendant, the president continues his questioning.

> PRESIDENT: Tell us a little about what criterion guided you in choosing which painting to take.
> ACCUSED: Quality. Artistic value. I could have taken . . . a Raphael, a Titian, a Correggio. But *La Gioconda* was the real treasure—the perfect painting to restore to Italy.

PRESIDENT: You didn't think of the higher price *La
Gioconda* would bring?

ACCUSED: No, never. Also, more than any of the other
paintings, *La Gioconda* lent itself to being stolen
because of its size.

PRESIDENT: How come, then, that you wrote your
family that you had finally found the road to fortune—a fortune which you hoped to obtain . . .
when you returned to Paris for the second time?

ACCUSED [discomfited]: When I wrote that, I intended
to show ambition, nothing else . . .

PRESIDENT: But did you not write finally that you
grasped fortune in your hands?

ACCUSED: What do you expect, Signore Presidente?
Even though I was returning the *Mona Lisa* to
Italy without thought of profit, I hoped for *some-
thing.*

Barilli discusses with Perugia his relationships with
his fellow workmen in Paris. Vincenzo refers to their jokes
at his expense, their taunts, the fact that they "salted my
wine." Then the president brings up the visit to London.

PRESIDENT: Is it true that you tried to sell *La
Gioconda* in England?

Vincenzo grows agitated, almost enraged. He clenches
his fists, his eyes dart over the crowd of lawyers and
journalists, as though seeking the one responsible for this
slander.

ACCUSED: Me? I offered to sell the *Gioconda* to the
English? Who says so? It's false! Who says so? Who
wrote that?

PRESIDENT: But it is you yourself who said so, during
one of your examinations which I have right here in
front of me.

ACCUSED: I said it? Who wrote those lies? Vignol,
perhaps? [M. François Vignol, a commissioner of
the French police, was assigned to assist in Perugia's

examination.] Or was it our "friend," Geri?
[Laughter in court.]
PRESIDENT: No, not at all. It's the deposition you gave
before the examining magistrate.

Vincenzo continues to profess disbelief and amaze-
ment. He is, of course, fighting to preserve an altruistic
role which will be destroyed if the London accusation is
made to stick. He asserts that he didn't go to England to
sell the *Mona Lisa* but simply "for amusement, with some
friends."

PRESIDENT: Then did you or did you not take steps to
sell the *Gioconda*?
ACCUSED: I did not. Only, passing by a postcard shop
and seeing several photographs of *La Gioconda,* it
occurred to me to ask the advice of an antiques
dealer about the best way to return the portrait to
Italy. Nothing but that . . . The antiquarian
advised me instead to return the painting to France.
Useless advice. . . .

Vincenzo continues with great emphasis:

French gold could never corrupt me! I took the
painting for Italy, and back to Italy I would bring
it—at any cost!
PRESIDENT: Nevertheless, your unselfishness wasn't
total—you did expect *some* benefit from restora-
tion.
ACCUSED: Ah benefit, benefit—certainly something
better than what happened to me here.
[Laughter in court.]
PRESIDENT: How did Geri's name come to your mind?
ACCUSED: "Friend" Geri's name? I read it in a news-
paper.
PRESIDENT: You proposed to Geri to convince the
Italian government to pay you half a million lire?
ACCUSED: That too is a lie! It was Geri who proposed
the deal to *me,* not I to him! Geri literally said to

me, "Let matters be—you'll see that it will go well
for all three of us."

PRESIDENT: Who was the third party?

ACCUSED: Commissioner Poggi, the director of the
Galleries. Believe me, Signore Presidente, what Geri
says is all a pose!

Perugia's indignation on the point seems genuine, and
after a few more questions in the same vein he is told to
resume his seat. The next witness, Police Chief Tarantelli,
describes the arrest of Perugia at the Hotel Tripoli-Italia
and his subsequent protests and statements when brought
to the station house. The chief is followed by Giovanni
Poggi of the Uffizi, who testifies to his discussions with
Geri, the letters from Perugia and finally their visit to the
hotel to inspect the painting. Poggi remains dignified, detached, a shade evasive.

PRESIDENT: Did you speak of remuneration?

POGGI: No. I limited myself to telling Perugia that
I would have to notify the Minister and the Department of the Belle Arti in Rome . . . On the
point of leaving, he begged me to conclude the
arrangements quickly.

PRESIDENT: Did not Perugia speak to you about a
price?

POGGI: No, I don't think so.

PRESIDENT: Then did he speak of a reward?

POGGI: No. He didn't speak to me about either, if I
remember correctly. We only agreed that I would
have charge of the painting, and in the meantime
I would write to the Minister to notify him of the
discovery. . . .

To persistent questioning by Barilli, Poggi again re-
sponds that no definitive prices had been discussed—then
recalls that Geri *did* hint at a request for two million lire.
The defense lawyers, Carena and Targetti, elicit from
Poggi that Perugia was cooperative and trusting, that he

seemed to be "a sincere person." Professor Paolo Amaldi, the psychological consultant, interjects a question.

AMALDI: What impression did you have at this time of Perugia's emotional state?
POGGI: He seemed moved by these events, but without displaying any outward sign or any abnormalities.

The next witness, Professor Nello Tarchiani, a prominent art expert, testifies to the value of the painting and explains how identification of the panel was arrived at. He notes that it was based on photographs as well as the official stamp of the Louvre on the back. Poggi also participates in the colloquy.

CARENA: Is it possible to falsify a stamp?
POGGI: Yes. But I must point out that our identification was complete because of these circumstances: In the painting there were several slight cracks, and these were verified. More important . . . is that another stamp, from the Museum of Versailles, was found on the painting. This particular mark is not mentioned in any catalogue and is known only to the curator of the Louvre.

(What was generally overlooked by the court and various official reports was a small, significant fact: once the genuine panel had been stolen from the Louvre, and the back could be examined at leisure, it would have been the simplest thing in the world to duplicate on a forgery any and all stamps or secret marks found there. While this would not apply to the Chaudron copies sent overseas *before* the theft, it obviously bears on any deception attempted during the years in which the *Mona Lisa* was in hiding.)

Following Tarchiani's testimony, the French commissioner, François Vignol, is questioned through an interpreter. He corroborates earlier statements by Perugia, plus facts about the workman's life in Paris and duties at the Louvre.

> PRESIDENT: Can you indicate for us whether the paintings can be easily removed, and which of them is the most valuable?
>
> VIGNOL: All the paintings at the Louvre can be easily removed from the walls. The most valuable painting in that room was indeed the *Mona Lisa*.
>
> PERUGIA [jumping up]: I would have you notice that the painting of the *Gioconda* was also the smallest!

After a few more minor exchanges, the antiques dealer, Alfredo Geri, is called. Perugia glowers at him. Geri testifies to facts already brought out in court and again affirms that Perugia had set his own price. Perugia jumps up and asks permission to make a statement, and Barilli agrees.

> ACCUSED: When I came to Florence and was in Geri's presence, these were my exact words: "I want nothing; I set no price on the restitution I am making to Italy. Let them do it, and what they do will be well done." Then Geri said to me, "We'll do things in such a way as to make us all content." . . . And later he suggested to me, "You must say that you expect 500,000 lire, and you'll see that everything will go by itself in the best way possible."

Geri protests these comments, and Vincenzo counters with "He's lying!" The president intervenes and calms everyone down.

> ACCUSED: I repeat again . . . Geri said to me, "Insist on 500,000 lire, and you'll see that it will be given to you."
>
> GERI: On the second day we met, what did you say to me?
>
> ACCUSED: Me? Nothing.

> GERI: But you must remember that in the Piazza
> della Signoria you asked about the *reward* you
> expected.
> ACCUSED: That's not true!

Again a loud debate breaks out between the two men;
as *La Nazione* reports, "One asserts and the other denies."
Finally, Barilli calls a halt to the wrangling, admonishes
them both, and excuses Geri.

The next and final witness is the psychiatrist, Professor
Amaldi, called by the defense. He confirms his earlier
diagnosis that Perugia is neither an idiot nor an imbecile,
but concludes tactfully that he is "intellectually deficient."
He is then asked by Carena if he considers Vincenzo truly
responsible for his actions.

> AMALDI [judiciously]: I found that I had to ask my-
> self three questions: Is Perugia responsible for the
> act he committed? Is he partly responsible? Or is he
> completely irresponsible? I think that we may con-
> sider Perugia to be—semi-responsible.

On this brilliant sophism the session ends, and court
is adjourned until later that afternoon.

The final session of the hearing was devoted to closing
statements by the various attorneys. Bartoli, the prosecutor,
took issue with Professor Amaldi, contending that Perugia
should be held fully responsible—that he had acted with
premeditation and that the theft showed intelligence. (In
this respect he was correct, though the intelligence wasn't
Perugia's.) He also rejected Vincenzo's claim that he had
acted out of patriotism. The true motive, Bartoli insisted,
was plain and simple greed. In conclusion, he asked the
court to impose a sentence of three years.

Carena spoke first for the defense. He sketched in
Perugia's early years, mentioning that he had had to earn
his living from the age of twelve. He minimized the other

arrests as minor infractions; the workman, he said, was not a professional thief, but a simple, well-meaning, gentle person and an affectionate son. He had been misguided, nothing more—and now Carena asked the judges to return Vincenzo to his family in Dumenza. Targetti spoke next and again insisted that the entire trial was illegal, since the crime had been committed on foreign soil where Italy had no jurisdiction. He argued that Perugia's actions had been purely, if mistakenly, in reprisal against the French, and not for personal gain. By freeing the prisoner, he declared to the judges, "you will have listened to the voices that are coming from every part of Italy, where there is nobody who desires the condemnation of the accused!" At this ringing declaration, the spectators broke into cheers and applause, and Perugia, wiping away his tears, embraced his attorneys warmly.

So the great trial ended, with no references whatever to the Lancelottis or the elusive diary, or to the occasional rumors that still arose linking the carpenter's act somehow to a mysterious "master swindler."

As for Vincenzo Perugia, he had played his role to the hilt and carried it off; yet he didn't succeed with everyone. An observer for Rome's *La Tribuna* noted with considerable acuity:

> To observe him, one would think he had nothing to do with the trial. He displayed temper when he felt the witnesses were not testifying accurately, but it was a superficial display. Not for one moment was he disturbed. . . . Either he has never believed that he has committed a crime or he has indulged so much in autosuggestion that he has lost all sense of the importance of it.

The next day the tribunal reconvened; then President Barilli announced that, taking all factors into consideration, the judges had agreed on a sentence for Perugia of one year and fifteen days. While the courtroom buzzed with talk, Vincenzo was handcuffed and led off to the Murate lost in thought, and one reporter noted that his expression resembled "*Mona Lisa*'s enigmatic smile."

At the end of July, Perugia's lawyers asked for another hearing to appeal the sentence. The carpenter was now somewhat thinner and paler, but still obdurate. To observers he seemed to waver, as though about to make a revelatory statement. Then he rallied. Speaking slowly in a low voice, he repeated that he had brought the Leonardo to Italy to enrich the Uffizi and the city of Florence. "I insist on this point," he said. "Of the rest, little interests me."

Pleas for a pardon or a reduction were presented by the defense attorneys, and after deliberation the court voted to reduce Perugia's sentence to seven months. Since he had already been in prison for seven months plus nine days, he was ordered released on the spot. So on July 29, 1914, Vincenzo found himself penniless, purposeless—and free.

Leaving the courthouse with his jubilant lawyers, he was hardly aware of the handshakes and pats on the back from well-wishers and reporters. None of that mattered to him any longer. Almost three years had gone by, the great gamble was over, the painting was in the Salon Carré; he and the madonna were both back where they had started.

"Where will you go now?" Targetti asked him.

Perugia shrugged. "Home to Dumenza, but not right away. I'm tired; tonight I'll go to that little hotel where I stayed when I first came here."

"You'll have a surprise," the lawyer said. "It's not the Tripoli-Italia any more. They changed the name to the Hotel La Gioconda."

PART SIX

The Riddle

. . . With a Leonard going cheap
If it should prove, as promised,
That Joconde
Whereof a copy contents the Louvre.

—ROBERT BROWNING,
The Ring and the Book

27

WHEN THE *Mona Lisa* came back to Paris in January 1914, one of the café songs celebrating her return struck a gloomy but prescient note. The entertainers sang:

> "It's me, I'm the *Gioconda*—
> Wait for the varnish to crumble,
> Wait for the end of the world,
> I'll smile beneath the bombs . . ."

In June of that year, some three weeks after Perugia's trial, a Serbian fanatic named Gavrilo Princip shot and killed Archduke Franz Ferdinand, heir to the Hapsburg throne, and his wife the Duchess of Hohenberg. One month later—the day before Vincenzo stepped from the Murate a free man—Austria declared war on Serbia; other nations soon followed, and on midnight of August 4 the entry of Great Britain made the European conflict general.

When Princip pulled the trigger of his Browning pistol in Sarajevo he also triggered a devastating world war which, Barbara Tuchman notes, acted "like a band of scorched earth dividing that time from ours." In that great disaster scores of lesser events were eclipsed, and among the bits and pieces of misplaced history was the curious chronicle of Valfierno, Chaudron, Perugia, and Lisa del Giocondo. This prewar caprice, like so many others, was swept aside by far more serious matters, but Lisa's story didn't end there. Nor is it over yet.

The *Mona Lisa,* now safe in the Louvre under the firm protection of its curators, has left behind it a gaudy trail of romance and mystery. No other painting in history has ever been so written about, debated, praised, analyzed, scorned, acclaimed, evaluated, studied, puzzled over or generally mythicized. And though this work is more than four and a half centuries old, it is still marked by odd paradoxes, unanswered questions, enigmas, contradictions, challenges, denials, claims and counterclaims.

Some of these puzzles go back to Leonardo's time, others are fairly recent—all are relevant today. Later, various answers and explanations will be offered; but first a few baffling ambiguities can be considered.

La Gioconda is no longer a painting but a cultural icon; its hagiography is varied, and even its origins are in doubt. Uncertainty has cloaked this story from the beginning, as Roy McMullen wrote: "The panel is unsigned and undated. There are no traces of a commission, no records of payments, and no recognizable allusions to the work in the fairly abundant Italian correspondence of the early 1500's." Most scholars believe that da Vinci, the quintessential Renaissance man, began the portrait in Florence in 1502 or 1503 and, apparently obsessed with it, carried it with him for many years. But who was his model —the mysterious woman who sat for him and occupied his thoughts for so long? Since Leonardo left no notes or sketches dealing with this project, all our information must come from other sources. The earliest clue is from Antonio de Beatis, secretary to Cardinal Louis of Aragon. Beatis wrote that in October 1517 the eminent cardinal visited Leonardo's studio, where the painter showed him "three pictures: one of a certain Florentine lady, done from life at the insistence of the late Magnificent, Giuliano de' Medici, another of Saint John the Baptist as a young man, and one of the Madonna and the Child . . . and all of them most perfect . . ." Was this "certain Florentine lady" the *Gioconda*—a paramour perhaps of Lorenzo de' Medici's son, Giuliano?

The next mention of the painting comes from da Vinci's biographer, Giorgio Vasari, who wrote in 1550:

> For Francesco del Giocondo, Leonardo undertook to execute a portrait of his wife, Mona Lisa. He worked on this painting for four years, and then left it unfinished; and today it is in the possession of King Francis of France, at Fontainebleau. If one wanted to see how faithfully art can imitate nature, one could readily perceive it from this head; for here Leonardo subtly reproduced every living detail.

"Mona" was at the time simply a short form of "madonna" or "madame"—and Vasari's clear reference would seem to settle the matter; but it doesn't. Historians noted that Lisa was born in Florence in 1479 and at the age of sixteen married a wealthy merchant named Francesco di Bartolomeo di Zanobi del Giocondo, nineteen years older than herself. This means that she would have been only twenty-three or twenty-four years old when Leonardo started his painting, yet most observers feel the Louvre portrait definitely shows an older woman. Estimates of the *Gioconda*'s age run from "early thirties" to "fortyish," and as one art dealer pointed out, "If anything, da Vinci would have made her look *younger* than she was, to please his patron."

Equally puzzling, why did Vasari refer to the portrait as being in an "unfinished" state? The same language appears in the reputable Baedeker guide to Paris for 1907, which says, "Leonardo worked four years on this painting and then left it unfinished"; but even the most cursory glance at the panel shows it to be as complete and finished a work as any in the museum.

In describing the lady's features, Vasari went into rhapsodies:

The eyes had their natural luster and moistness, and . . . pearly tints that demand the greatest delicacy of execution. The eyebrows were completely natural, growing thickly in one place and lightly in another. . . . The nose was finely painted, with rosy and delicate nostrils as in life. The mouth, joined to the flesh tints of the face by the red of the lips, appeared to be living flesh rather than paint.

Now the discrepancies become more obvious. All this toothsome sensuality might indeed fit a lady in the bloom of her Florentine youth, but it hardly describes the worldly, mature, sallow doyenne who surveys her visitors from the wall of the Louvre. The *Mona Lisa*'s eyebrows do not grow thickly—she has none at all—and even if we allow for a degree of fading plus numerous layers of ancient varnish, of rosy nostril and red lip there is hardly a trace.

Surprisingly, in the inventory of Francis's royal collection at Fontainebleau, the portrait is listed simply as "A courtesan in a gauze veil," and there are no references in this carefully kept record to Madame Lisa or to her husband who presumably commissioned the work.

Art expert Sir Kenneth Clark theorizes that the subject had a deep psychological hold over da Vinci, embodying "something inherent in his vision." How else, he asked, could one explain the fact "that while he was refusing commissions from Popes, Kings and Princesses he spent his utmost skill and, we are told, three years in painting the second wife of an obscure Florentine citizen?" The answer may be that the sitter was in fact someone else, with special meaning for the genius from Vinci. There are various possibilities. One contender is Isabella d'Este, the Marchioness of Mantua, who had a long close relationship with Leonardo. At the time he began his portrait Isabella was thirty years old, an age which fits the model reasonably. A second candidate is Costanza d'Avalos, the Duchess of Francaville. Like Isabella, Costanza was a

Renaissance beauty of great style and intelligence, a "liberated woman," and for a while the governor of the island of Ischia. This duchess, who would have been in her early forties, was shrewd, forceful, self-confident—qualities that seem to mirror the spirit of *La Joconde.*

Another notion, attempting to resolve the problem, is that Leonardo painted similar portraits of *two different models.* One of these was Lisa del Giocondo and the other, in the same pose, depicted Isabella of Aragon, the young Duchess of Milan who became a mistress of the Medici nobleman mentioned by the cardinal's secretary. However, there is no real evidence to back up any of these candidates.

Other theories about the subject are more bizarre. Among them:

The *Mona Lisa* is a *finzione*—a clever sham; she has no identity, but is a composite of various elegant, highborn women whom Leonardo idealized.

The portrait is of an attractive young man with whom da Vinci was infatuated; the artist painted his lover this way as a transvestite joke.

The panel shows a courtesan of Naples, who appealed to Leonardo because of her aristocratic manner.

The lady (whoever she may be) is definitely pregnant, as shown by the slightly swollen hands and face, and her "self-satisfied expression."

Even Sigmund Freud had his say, claiming that the portrait and its smile were a form of psychic catharsis for Leonardo. In an essay in 1910, the psychologist stated that da Vinci was really dealing with "the intensity of the erotic relations between mother and child."

All these speculations aside, the fact is that the *Mona Lisa*—or more accurately, A *Mona Lisa*—wound up in the collection of King Francis I and was hung in his favorite château at Fontainebleau. Vincenzo Perugia was completely wrong; the *Gioconda* wasn't stolen from Italy by Bonaparte, but was fairly acquired by the French King.

During the last years of his life, Leonardo stayed in the Château de Cloux as a guest of Francis I, his patron and enthusiastic admirer. In that period he sold or gave the *Mona Lisa* to Francis—or it may have been presented to the King by the artist's heir and devoted pupil, Francesco Melzi.

Legend says that the portrait was placed in Francis's bathroom, but this is a distortion. At Fontainebleau the King's *appartement des bains* was a large cultural and recreational complex, resembling the ancient baths of Rome, and the elegant walls of this "bathroom" were adorned with many fine paintings—not only the Leonardo, but also works by Raphael, Giulio Romano and Andrea del Sarto. There the *Mona Lisa* remained for years, admired by royal visitors, praised by Europe's connoisseurs and, incidentally, copied by talented artists and students trying to emulate the great master.

Late in the 1600s, Louis XIV took the *Mona Lisa* to Versailles. His successor, Louis XV, disliked the portrait intensely and banished it to the apartment of the palace superintendent. During the French Revolution, it was hidden with other royal possessions in a warehouse near the Place de la Concorde. Later it was rescued by Napoleon —who indeed appreciated its beauty—and placed in his bedroom in the Palace of the Tuileries; and from there it went finally to the Grande Galerie of the Louvre. During the Franco-Prussian War, the painting was taken for safekeeping to the arsenal of Brest. Afterward it was returned to Paris and hung in the museum's Salon Carré, where it stayed until its fateful meeting with Perugia and the Lancelottis.

The return of the errant *Joconde* to her rightful place in the Carré should have brought her story to a satisfying end; on the contrary, it launched a new chain of events and set off waves of speculation which persist—to the annoyance of the Louvre's curators—until this day.

In September 1928, Diana Rice, art critic for *The New York Times,* observed that after the painting was recovered "there started a series of *Mona Lisa* tales that still continue. Every imaginable reason has been set forth to prove that the returned painting is spurious."

Is the *Mona Lisa* spurious? To find an answer, we must step further into the maze.

28

ART THEFT is big business; experts say that today it's the second largest source of crime income, exceeded only by narcotics. Though a priceless number escape for good, many stolen works of art are eventually traced and recovered; and when these finally go back to their owners they're welcomed gladly and without question. But this wasn't the case with the *Gioconda,* who came back to Paris trailing much doubt and uncertainty. In short, her long-awaited return didn't put an end to the stories and speculations.

Long before the Marqués put his plan into operation, there were rumors that *La Joconde* had been snatched from the Louvre. According to these stories, the theft had taken place years earlier and had been hushed up. As for the picture, some said it was eventually ransomed and returned to the Carré wall. Others claimed that it disappeared and later was secretly replaced by a facsimile.

Such rumors were never substantiated, but they have kept surfacing with great persistence—repeated almost as gospel by people as diverse as a language professor in

Rome, a journalist in Grasse, an antique-book dealer in New York City, a gallery owner in Pasadena.

Back in 1911, while Paris was reeling over the lost *Joconde, La Patrie* claimed that the painting had actually been stolen in 1903, and that a copy had been substituted. As a result, the writer added, "Doubt is growing about the authenticity of the stolen *Mona Lisa.*" And a full year before Perugia made his move, a reporter for *Cri de Paris* stirred up a storm by insisting that he had seen the real *Joconde* in the hands of an art dealer named Louis Heuzy, on the Rue St. Étienne. Later (perhaps under official pressure) the editors recanted, giving the odd excuse that they had printed their story merely to arouse the public over the poor security at the Louvre.

During their meeting in Morocco in 1914, Valfierno and Decker discussed all this, and the Marqués denied any personal knowledge of an earlier Louvre heist. He did repeat, however, that there *were* other *Mona Lisa*s in the world and that he and Chaudron had "merely added to the gross total."

Then, when the picture resurfaced in Florence and Perugia was arrested, the rumors began, if anything, to multiply. In Brussels, *L'Étoile Belgique* reported that a Dutch antiques dealer, Jacob van Pardoek, had strongly questioned the authenticity of the found portrait. Van Pardoek insisted that it was simply a good fake which had been offered him months earlier, through an intermediary in London. Other newspapers devoted space to this and similar tales which added to the mystery and prompted art historian René Schneider to write in 1923: "To want something definitive on 'La Joconde,' given the present state of our knowledge, is to go around her in circles."

As the years passed, these circles became ever-widening ripples of fact and legend, and no search for the real *Mona Lisa* can be meaningful without mentioning some of them.

In November 1926 readers of *The New York Times* were surprised to find:

"MONA LISA" YARN
STARTLES ALL PARIS

The Parisian art world was thrown into a high state of emotion by the assertion of a well-known critic that "La Joconde" . . . by Leonardo da Vinci, one of the most famous masterpieces in the world, has never actually been returned to the Louvre since its theft on Aug. 21, 1911, but was replaced with a clever copy. . . .

The charge was made by art critic Emanuel Bourcier of *L'Oeuvre,* who announced that a replica of the *Joconde* had been substituted during its railway trip from Florence to Paris. And what had become of the genuine portrait? Bourcier said it was in the hands of a Paris dealer, Édouard Jonas, who had it hidden in the basement of his shop on the Place Vendôme. When questioned, the dealer stated that he was acting on behalf of the maritime governor of Toulon, Admiral Patou, and that Bourcier was correct. The Toulon portrait had been offered earlier to art dealers Bonnat and Duveen, and—inevitably—to Pierpont Morgan.

Jonas at the time also had a gallery in New York, on East Fifty-seventh Street. In December, landing in the U.S. on the liner *Rochambeau,* he was besieged by reporters and changed his story somewhat. The Admiral's painting was perhaps not *the* da Vinci, but still the two pictures were "identical in size, coloring, and in fact every detail."

The dealer and his claims gradually faded from notice, but the following year a controversial art pamphlet made the rounds in Paris. It theorized that Francis I had had an exact copy made of the *Mona Lisa* while at Fontainebleau and had presented it to a court favorite. The writer claimed that it was this version, not the original, which had been placed in the Louvre after the robbery. The pamphlet had some earmarks of a Valfierno stunt, since it was similar to the faked news items he had formerly created; any victim worried about the validity of the picture he had bought from the Marqués would obviously draw comfort from a brochure of this nature.

The next bombshell landed in August 1933, when *The Sunday Express* in London ran a large headline:

NEW RIDDLE OF WORLD'S
MOST FAMOUS PICTURE

Man Who Stole Mona Lisa Says
Painting in the Louvre Is a Fake

The mystery man in this story was the British swindler Jack Dean, who had gone to the French Embassy in London and confessed that he had been part of the original Vafierno team. According to Dean (who never expained his sudden rush of penitence), he had worked with Perugia, helping to steal and hide the panel. Later he and a "friend" managed in secret to switch the portrait with a forgery which had been prepared but never sent abroad; and Perugia had then carried the forgery to Florence in his trunk, under the mistaken impression that it was the da Vinci. Now the roller-coaster takes a fast twist: growing worried about being caught with the priceless *Mona Lisa,* Dean and his accomplice decided to unload the hot picture as quickly as possible on a Paris art dealer. They did so, for a modest fee, by assuring the dealer that it was a *fine facsimile.*

The unsuspecting dealer, Dean claimed, sold the portrait to a French collector for his villa in Algiers; and several years later while in Algiers, Dean supposedly went to this man's home to satisfy his curiosity. "There it was," he told the *Express,* "in his gallery. He has got Leonardo da Vinci's *Mona Lisa,* and thinks he has only a wonderful copy."

Dean's switched panel became known among journalists as the *"Joconde* of Algiers," but his story is highly apocryphal and was angrily disputed by French officials such as Henri Verne, director of national museums, and Émile Bollaërt, director of the Beaux-Arts. Bollaërt mentioned that Dean had made an appointment with him to discuss the matter and had never showed up. He strongly denounced the tale, calling it "as mythical as a sea serpent." The director pointed out that the Louvre painting had been examined and validated by the foremost experts of France, and added, "There is no room for doubt: the *Joconde* stolen in 1911 is indeed the one which was recovered in 1913." His statement would appear conclusive if we overlook theories to the effect that the portrait "stolen in 1911" may not have been by the gifted hand of Leonardo!

Yet another mystery surfaced in October 1949, in Houston, Texas—for Valfierno in the old days a fruitful hunting ground. In Tours, *La Nouvelle République* published a story under the heading:

THE REAL MONA LISA
Of Leonardo da Vinci
Will Not Be Found in the Louvre
But in the United States

The report said that the Marquis Donald D'Orley, an "expert on paintings," had just exhibited in Houston a portrait which he claimed was the real *Gioconda.* The Marquis said he had recently brought the portrait from Switzerland at the request of its present owner, Mme. Vivian Guénod-Lyle, and that "contrary to the assertions of the Louvre . . . the authentic 'Mona Lisa' " was now in his possession. D'Orley and his portrait bobbed up for a

while in different parts of the U.S. Southwest, then
dropped from public view.

In 1958, Chicago journalist M. W. Newman revived
the Perugia story and again speculated as to the portrait's
authenticity. Since then other items and reports have also
appeared, raising questions as to the bona fides of the
masterpiece which was welcomed back to the Salon Carré
with such rejoicing.

Understandably, today's Louvre curators react to these
challenges with great and abiding indignation: members of
the museum's official family, on all levels, have no doubts
as to the legitimacy of their prize.

Madeleine Hours, *grande dame* of the Louvre and
Chef des services du laboratoire, has published numerous
articles on da Vinci's painting techniques, and was placed
in charge of the portrait when it came to the United States
on a famous goodwill tour in 1963. Mme. Hours, com-
bative as well as knowledgeable, bridled at the mere
thought that there might be anything amiss with the
Louvre's *Mona Lisa.* "In the last thirty years," she announced, her chin jutting, "I have never seen a painting
of *La Joconde* which could *ever* have been by Leonardo,
except the one here in our collection."

The forceful *directrice,* known to the late President
John F. Kennedy as "the little sister of the *Mona Lisa*" (a
more tactful label than Lyndon Johnson's reference to her
as "the *Mona Lisa*'s mother") obviously bases her judgment on impeccable expertise plus a deep inner response
which is real if indefinable: "It is something one feels, one
senses. I can tell now by looking at a picture whether it's
a Leonardo, yes or no. The subtle modeling of the features,
the beautiful hands, the moods, the smiles—nobody else
painted that way; the craftsmanship is unmistakable."

She is seconded by Mme. Faillant-Dumas, director of
museum documentation, who has on file a variety of X rays
and chemical analyses used to authenticate the Louvre's

madonna. "The *Mona Lisa* is in its own category," she asserts, "an absolutely remarkable example of the perfection of technique. No artist begins to compare with Leonardo; he could never be duplicated."

A veteran New York gallery owner, with many years of experience in the field, disagrees. "I can give you fifty artists today," he said, "who can make you excellent copies of the *Mona Lisa* right down to the last brush stroke."

The official Louvre position is generally accepted and endorsed—though not with vast enthusiasm—by most art historians. Among these experts is Bonnie Burnham, executive director of the International Foundation for Art Research, a prestigious clearinghouse which services museums, galleries and major dealers. The foundation maintains a large archive, providing information on art thefts, forgeries, the recovery of stolen goods, claims and litigations, and activities of organizations such as Interpol. Its experts also, on request, prepare special reports on the authenticity of works of art.

"No doubt the *Mona Lisa* has gone through a mythification process—especially since it came to the United States," says Mrs. Burnham. "Do you remember, we had those incredible lines in Washington and here in New York? Then later the same thing happened when it was on tour in Japan and the Soviet Union; it was a phenomenon —millions of people pouring out to see this one painting. I understand in Tokyo it became almost a mania."

Discussing the various claims and challenges, Mrs. Burnham smiles, her lively eyes flashing. "The idea of a substitute for the *Mona Lisa* is fascinating and charming; still, you know, it's not all that unique. There *is* a market —unfortunately a fairly big one—for stolen art. In fact, we run into cases where paintings and artifacts of mediocre quality can be upgraded and can actually bring a higher price if they're labeled as 'stolen' or 'smuggled.' Somehow that gives them cachet."

Writing in 1975 about the looting of monuments and
archaeological sites, Mrs. Burnham described a ploy which
echoes the deceptions of the enterprising Marqués:

> Another common practise in southeast Asia is for
> temple guardians to commission fakes of a sculptured
> lintel or figure which is part of their temple. When
> dealers come through on a buying trip, the temple
> guardian offers to sell the piece in question, saying
> that he will have it removed . . . and smuggled out to
> to dealer. The dealer departs, and is sent the copy
> made for the purpose.

Mrs. Burnham observed, "It has been pointed out that
perhaps the guardians have finally found a practical system
for saving their monuments."

In view of all this, did she not have a doubt or two
about the Louvre's masterpiece? The executive director
shook her head. "No, not really; it's much too well established. The true story of the portrait can be traced back
all the way to Francis I. So we do have its entire history
and provenance."

In general, the opinion of the art community is perhaps summed up by Joseph Veach Noble in the current
Macropaedia Britannica:

> At least a dozen excellent replicas of Leonardo da
> Vinci's "Mona Lisa" exist, many of them by his
> students. Various owners of these copies have at
> various times claimed that they possess the original.
> The Louvre is satisfied that it owns the painting by
> Leonardo because close examination reveals slight
> changes in composition underneath the outermost
> layer of paint, and because this painting has an un-
> broken record of ownership from the time that the
> artist painted it.

The reference to changes under the top paint layer is
murky: this may indeed tell us something about the age

of the various pigments, but it hardly offers a clue as to
who wielded the brushes. And the mention of an "un-
broken record of ownership" is a feeble case, since it omits
several crucial gaps. During the early 1700s the panel was
often shuttled between Versailles and Paris, and in 1870
it languished without much protection in the Brest arsenal.
It may even have been snatched from the Louvre as early as
1903, and its ownership certainly changed hands for twenty-
seven mysterious months when it remained under the aegis
of Vincenzo Perugia.

Despite X rays, microchemical analyses, carbon-dating
tests and the protestations of curators, the riddle of the
Gioconda persists, and its solution seems intertwined with
other paradoxes: Why, as late as 1907, did reports say that
the picture was never completed—and where now is this
"incomplete" portrait? Was a version of the *Mona Lisa*
completed *after* the artist's death, by Melzi or another of
da Vinci's disciples? If the portrait had been commissioned
by Signore del Giocondo, why did Leonardo cling to it
instead of delivering it in due course to the rightful buyer?

On a more contemporary level, other questions can
now be answered: How did this old and fragile wood
panel, after August 1911, survive two years of neglect
without warping or cracking? Did the Marqués have a paid
accomplice inside the Louvre or the Paris Prefecture at
the time of the robbery? And finally, what happened to
Yves Chaudron's forgeries?

29

JOHN WALKER, former director of the National Gallery of
Art, recalls the *Mona Lisa*'s official visit to America in
January 1963. Before that visit Mme. Hours, then head
of conservation, came to Washington, D.C., to help with

the arrangements. In his memoirs, Walker reports that
Mme. Hours and the staff of the Louvre were horrified at
sending the fragile painting on so long a voyage:

> She told me . . . that when a maniac a few years
> earlier had attacked the picture, she had taken it at
> once to her studio to see whether any damage had
> been done, and that because of the change of relative
> humidity, within a few hours the panel had curved
> and nearly broken; and finally that, as the x-rays she
> brought with her showed, there was an incipient split
> in the panel which if prolonged would run right
> through the celebrated smile.

Italian poplar, the support of the *Gioconda,* is a rela-
tively soft wood, and the aging/drying process makes it
highly vulnerable to cracking, warping, rot and infestation.
Walker too was alarmed and, like the Louvre officials, was
determined that, above all, "the painting must be protected
from any change of temperature and humidity." It traveled
from France to the United States in a special aluminum
case lined with Styrofoam and slotted to hold the panel
firmly. In the National Gallery in Washington and
later in New York's Metropolitan Museum of Art, air-
conditioning and humidity were fine-tuned on a twenty-
four-hour basis to simulate "the very air she had breathed
in Paris."

Today in the Louvre the panel hangs in its own glass-
enclosed alcove, with the air again as carefully controlled
and regulated as in a baby's incubator.

All of which leads to an inescapable puzzle: how could
this perishable work, already four centuries old in 1911,
have possibly survived the ravages of the theft without
showing the slightest trace of damage? At first the panel
was trotted rather carelessly about Paris, from the Rue
St.-Merri to the Rue Bichat to the Rue de l'Hôpital-St.-

Louis; then it received years of benign neglect in a trunk in the airless closet of a slum dwelling. From there it traveled in the dead of winter to Florence, where it was again shunted about before it finally went home. Yet none of this led to any of the severe cracking or warping so feared by the Louvre's conservators.

Mme. Hours can offer no ready explanation. "We have no way of knowing what the actual circumstances were, back then. In a case like this the greatest danger would come from sudden changes in humidity or temperature; and fortunately the panel stayed here in Paris for *most* of that time. Still . . ." She shrugged her shoulders and gazed out her window, as though seeking a solution in the green, sun-drenched gardens behind the Louvre.

What kind of atmospheric conditions were at work, shielding this ancient panel so well that, after all the neglect, it emerged without a scratch? Michael Varese, an expert restorer of furniture and antiques, has supplied the answer. "With strong changes in humidity," Varese points out, "wood fibers start coming apart—you might say the wood sort of 'goes beserk.' In 1960 the offices at the Louvre were most likely steam-heated, which is deadly for this kind of panel, because steam heat dries the air and quickly draws moisture from the wood. That's when the panel started to warp."

Varese believes that, back in 1911, the *Mona Lisa* was saved by a fairly steady humidity level: "Perugia's room might have had a small wood or coal grate, if anything, and this works to draw in new air and keep humidity constant." He points out that wood is an organic living substance, and that fibers begin to break down with the passing of time. "By 1960," he says, "another fifty years had gone by since the theft; the panel was more vulnerable, just as an aging person would be."

When Perugia hid the panel in the bottom of his

trunk, Varese adds, it was a wonderful stroke of luck, since the snug fit immobilized the panel, gave it rigidity, and supported it during the time it was out of its frame.

Another of the ongoing mysteries has to do with the fact that Vincenzo Perugia, alone of all the suspects, escaped the Paris investigators' net in the hectic weeks after the robbery. The periodical *L'Illustration* publicized this when Perugia was jailed, the editors again noting that a list of 257 suspects had been presented to Judge Drioux's office and forwarded to the fingerprint bureau. Everyone at the Louvre cooperated fully with Bertillon's fingerprinting plan; from the highest curators to the lowliest porters they had "agreed to place their fingers on the appropriate forms." But for reasons never explained, *only* Perugia was unlisted, and was spared a procedure which would have trapped him.

During the investigation Pierre Marcel, a professor at the École des Beaux-Arts, wrote to *Le Figaro* pinpointing the role of the glazier crews who came to the Louvre to build the shadow boxes in 1910. Marcel's letter said: ". . . for those who really know the museum, the glaziers are the only probable lead." An assistant curator named Guiffrey contacted the professor about this, and later they reminded investigators that all of the workmen's names could be found on pay sheets which they had signed at the time; in short, every man who had worked on the glass covers was identifiable from the pay records. A foreman in charge of the glazier crews was questioned in a desultory way, but apparently no further action was taken.

The editors of *Petit Parisien* also repeated that the Criminal Records Office had a complete dossier on Vincenzo Perugia, and wondered

> why no one at the Quai des Orfèvres thought to delve into this fellow's past—to ask whether M. Bertillon did not have anything on file about him. A mere

glance at the records would have been enough to
regard him as a suspicious character because of the
earlier offenses mentioned. The idea would then inevitably have arisen of . . . comparing his fingerprints
with those found on the frame of the *Mona Lisa,* and
of ordering a meticulous search of his residence . . .
instead of which he was merely asked a few questions,
and replied very collectedly . . . that he had not
worked at the museum during the seven months
before the theft.

The editors made another charge: in the matter of
checking fingerprints—something every security guard
and workman was supposed to undergo—Perugia had
actually been called in twice; but, "need we say, he didn't
bother to appear, he was not sent for, and there was no
order for him to be picked up and made to comply with
this essential formality."

The Criminal Records Office, in its report to the
Prefecture, laid all the responsibility at the door of M.
Hamard, director general of Sûreté investigations. *Petit
Parisien* also found witnesses to the fact that M. Hamard
"never went into the Criminal Records Office." The
journalists added, "Without a doubt it is this strange, total
lack of interest which enabled the robber . . . to escape
M. Bertillon's attention."

The same casualness marked the search for Perugia's
mystery woman, "Mathilde." She had been traced as far as
Nice, where she surely could have been found with no
great effort; and Deputy Niclausse had at first attached
"a great deal of importance to her evidence." An inspector
was sent to serve Mathilde with a subpoena to appear in
court in Paris, but after a halfhearted, ineffectual attempt
to locate her in the Nice-Monaco area the search was
dropped.

Was this "total lack of interest" purely accidental, or
was there a Perugia cover-up, extending not only to his

fingerprints but to his incriminating diary, which to this day is still unaccounted for?

After considering all these factors, it's my belief that Valfierno did have an undercover agent—probably someone working at the Police Prefecture rather than at the Louvre. In the Île de la Cité, too many leads were overlooked and too many opportunities strangely bungled. Admittedly this is speculation and at so late a date nothing can be proven, but the facts and the clues are compelling. Even the curious episode of Vincenzo's left thumbprint later came under fire: in 1913, a news report claimed that *other* fingerprints had also been found, but that officials couldn't say "which finger or which hand was involved," because the robber had leaned heavily on the glass and the fingerprints were "squashed." In view of all this, we might well ask whether or not the whole fingerprint search had been deliberately sabotaged.

Cover-ups are not a modern invention. In earlier schemes, Valfierno often used inside people—museum personnel, minor government officials and so on, who were susceptible to bribery and who, once implicated, would have remained cooperative. Given the risks and problems, it is feasible that the Marqués did have the help of at least one high police official when the *Mona Lisa* was stolen. Such a covert link would have protected the plan and bought valuable time for the gang to complete their sales of the six portraits by Chaudron.

Which brings us inevitably to the forgeries themselves, one of the abiding enigmas of this account.

The Chaudron replicas, like their elusive creator, have had a gift for anonymity, defying efforts to locate or identify them, and have now faded into the mass of extant *Mona Lisa* copies scattered by the hundreds throughout the world. Extended research involving contacts with art professionals in France, England and more than forty U. S. cities has produced much speculation but few viable leads—a tribute to the expertise of the master swindler who engineered the scheme so carefully and who covered his tracks so well afterwards.

The original buyers were men in their fifties or older who died years ago, and many details of this escapade died with them since their only safe course at the time was silence. What rich collector would voluntarily come forth to announce that he had bought the *Mona Lisa* under the impression that he was getting a "legitimate" masterpiece? And who among Valfierno's victims would have had the temerity later to demand his money back? The fine line between fact and conjecture has now grown blurred. However, it is presumed that one or two of the panels were destroyed by victims who realized that they'd been swindled and grew worried about the implications. Several panels also disappeared in the course of estate liquidations, at which point they would have drifted into the international network of art dealers, auctioneers, solicitors, salesmen, commission agents, antiquarians and curators. These exquisite facsimiles could well have inspired the claims of van Pardoek, Bourcier, Jonas, the Marquis D'Orley and others who insisted that they possessed, or knew the whereabouts of, the "real" *Gioconda*. And one or two Chaudrons may still be in the hands of innocent collectors, quite unaware of their bizarre history.

In the 1950s, France's leading authority on forged paintings, or *faux tableaux*, was Police Commissioner Guy Isnard, who spent many years trying to decipher this and other art riddles. In 1955 in Paris he helped organize an "International Show of Fakes in Art and History," and for one of the exhibits Isnard's staff rounded up no fewer than twelve respectable forgeries of the *Mona Lisa*! It is further believed that several of Isnard's twelve copies were from the brush of Yves Chaudron.

The commissioner launched a number of investigations of the da Vinci portrait and what he called "the

double mystery surrounding its origin and authenticity,"
and finally concluded that it was "hard to see any light
in this tangle."

M. Isnard also collated information on various extant
versions of the *Mona Lisa*—copies, McMullen wrote, "that
were thought worthy of scholarly attention." There are
today facsimiles of the *Gioconda* in French provincial collections at Mulhouse, Quimper, Bourg and Tours; also in
museums and collections as scattered as Leningrad, Oslo,
Innsbruck, Algiers and Stuttgart. A superior copy (though
without the background) is in the Prado Museum in
Madrid and has been attributed to an unknown Spanish
artist of the sixteenth century. Others are in the Torlonia
collection in Rome and the Walters Art Gallery in Baltimore; also in Miami Beach and Bologna, in Long Island's
Southampton and a bank vault in Switzerland. There is
even a version in the administrative offices of the Louvre
itself, making two copies of the portrait right in the same
museum! This *Joconde,* painted on canvas, hangs in a hall-
way of the Département des Peintures and is considered an
excellent replica dating from the seventeenth century.

In most—not all—of these cases, the portraits are
attributed not to Leonardo but to various students and
followers such as Francesco Melzi, Ambrogio da Predis,
Gian Caprotte ("Salai"), Antonio Boltraffio and Bernardino
Luini, as well as more recent fine artists such as Jean
Ducayer and Théodore Chassériau. There are also many
lesser copies created by workaday artists in the years before
the advent of full-color art reproduction techniques. These
portraits were sold by the score to tourists and minor collectors who wanted a *Mona Lisa* to grace the walls of their
homes.

Additionally, there is at present in Europe and America a small underground of stubborn claimants who firmly
believe that they own an actual portrait *painted by*

Leonardo; that their *Mona Lisa*s are not later copies but indeed genuine da Vincis, created by the master.

The portraits owned by these challengers are provably old, well documented, and in each case definitely predate the Valfierno copies. Of today's fascinating pretenders to the coveted throne of the *Joconde,* three in particular are worth mention.

30

ON A MILD SPRING DAY in 1944 Raymond Hekking was taking a stroll in the Riviera town of Grasse, and at the shop of a bric-a-brac dealer named Gaetan Watelot he noticed a pile of ancient dusty canvases. Hekking, a prominent antiques dealer in nearby Nice, poked through the paintings, came upon a copy of the *Mona Lisa,* and decided that he would like to own a secondhand *Joconde.* The Dutch dealer paid Watelot three thousand "old" francs (equivalent to about eight dollars), carried the picture home and cleaned it carefully.

To his surprise an exceptional portrait emerged, and the more Hekking looked at it the more convinced he became that this wasn't an ordinary copy but possibly a genuine Leonardo. The idea grew into an obsession with the elderly connoisseur, and as one local news report said, "Since then, Monsieur Hekking has had no aim in life but the affirming of his discovery."

In due time Raymond Hekking brought in experts and technicians and also won the support of his skeptical son, Jean. The painting from the junk shop was laced with a network of fine eggshell-type cracks—a *craquelure* which Hekking claimed was typical of the da Vinci period. He also concluded that the picture had originally been on a wooden panel but that sometime in the nineteenth century the wood became worm-eaten and the picture was transferred to canvas.

Such a technique, difficult and painstaking, does exist and was invented in the 1700s by a French art restorer named Picault. Another celebrated da Vinci, *Madonna with the Flower,* now in the Hermitage Museum in Leningrad, was transferred to canvas by this method when the original wood deteriorated.

The transfer process doesn't, as might be supposed, involve lifting the outer surface away from the old wood or canvas. Just the opposite. First this fragile surface—the painted picture—is completely covered with strips of facing paper or fabric, impregnated with a paraloid substance, to protect and reinforce the thin crust of pigment. The picture is then laid face down, sometimes floating on a bed of gelatin, and the defective backing is slowly cut, sliced and scraped away until the underlying gesso primer appears. A strong mesh fabric is affixed to this gesso base, and the layer of paint is now ready to be glued to a new support. After that, the fabric strips reinforcing the front of the picture are carefully removed.

The Hekkings have X rays which they claim show traces of the former wood grain, but experts have never agreed on this point. Chief among those who examined the *"Joconde* of Nice" was Milan's noted critic/historian Giorgio Nicodemi. Hekking said later that Professor Nicodemi believed the portrait to be by the master, but the art expert firmly denied this. Interviewed in 1962, Nicodemi commented, "I remember very well having seen in Nice, at the home of a cultured and courteous gentleman, a painting resembling the *Gioconda.* . . . I recall having remarked on the importance of the painting, even in comparison with numerous better-known copies of the famous work, and having said that the artist could properly be sought among the French masters of the early

sixteenth century." Which would indicate that it was
painted after da Vinci's death, while the *Mona Lisa* was at
Fontainebleau.

However, Hekking *père* stuck to his guns, repeating
his claim and pointing out, "Of course my *Gioconda* is
younger; it was painted first, and by the time Leonardo
painted the other one the model had aged." It was also
rumored that shipping magnate Aristotle Onassis planned
to buy the portrait from the Hekking family for $2 million,
but the sale never materialized.

Today this controversial picture is in the care of
Raymond Hekking's grandson, Patrice, who lives with his
own family in a handsome villa in Nice. Patrice retells
the story of his grandfather's discovery and his father's
efforts to validate the find. He also refers to the rumor, encountered at other times, that the *Mona Lisa* stolen in
1911 might not be the one currently in the Louvre. Having
examined his portrait with care, I can report that it is an
impressive work, and obviously—from the cracks, condition of the canvas, and the stretchers—of considerable age.
The model's expression is subtle, the colors are rich, there
is even a hint of Vasari's much admired rosy lips. However,
the background is very crude and, in my opinion, could
never have been executed by Leonardo. One other crucial
factor largely disqualifies the Hekking contender and
will be described shortly.

"After the publicity about our picture," Patrice
Hekking recalls, "we received many letters from other
people who owned copies of the *Joconde;* but none of
them made our claims as to provenance." How the portrait
came to Grasse is something of a mystery; Watelot the
bric-a-brac dealer knew only that he had acquired the
entire lot of old canvases when the basement of a mansion
was cleared out, but he could remember none of the
details.

Pressed further, Patrice said, "In my opinion, our

painting is definitely from the atelier of Leonardo da
Vinci, if not by himself." As to the famous lady in Paris,
Hekking shrugged. "Well, it would of course be impossible for the Louvre people to admit that theirs was a
fake." He smiled engagingly. "Anyway, we just don't argue
about the *Mona Lisa* in France."

While the Hekkings were promoting their cause in
Nice, another collector was championing his in London.
The late Henry F. Pulitzer, of the distinguished Pulitzer
family, acquired a version of the *Gioconda* in 1962 and
stated unequivocally that it was a genuine Leonardo. He
felt so strongly about this that at his own expense he published an elaborate one-hundred-page book filled with
news reprints, letters, analyses, X rays, color photographs
and commentaries by experts.

Pulitzer's portrait, known as the "Isleworth version,"
was mentioned in the 1951 *Encyclopedia Americana:*

> Since no original sketch exists for the *Mona Lisa,*
> it is not thought improbable that da Vinci first
> painted one portrait directly on canvas before work-
> ing on the final copy. The Isleworth version, in
> England, is admitted by many to be more beautiful
> than the Louvre painting.

The Pulitzer madonna can be traced back to the collection of the English portrait painter Sir Joshua Reynolds,
who lived and worked in the eighteenth century. The
picture was next acquired by Earl Brownlow of Somerset,
and in 1906 E. W. Gregory, writing in *The Connoisseur,*
compared the work favorably to the one in the Louvre and
the version in the Prado Museum. He called it "the beautiful picture by Leonardo da Vinci" and added, "Sir Joshua
[Reynolds] held the opinion that the French Gioconda
was not genuine, and many others to whom the three works
are familiar share his view."

Later it was purchased by the Isleworth collector

Hugh Blaker, whose stepfather, John Eyre, did a study of the painting entitled "The Two Mona Lisas." After being shown for some years at the Leicester Galleries, it passed to a Swiss art syndicate and was bought in 1962 by Henry Pulitzer. The price was never revealed, but to raise the needed funds Pulitzer admitted, "I had to sacrifice a large number of paintings in my collection and a house with all its contents. But to realize this dream no sacrifice was too much." In his book he then claimed: "The lady in question is no other than the long lost *Mona Lisa*, which . . . is not the picture in the Louvre . . . known mistakenly by this name until now. I am convinced that my lady was painted by Leonardo da Vinci in his studio."

There is no cynicism or deviousness in this lady of Pulitzer's; she smiles at the viewer with a gracious expression, and is decidedly the most youthful of the contenders. The face and hands of this young madonna are exquisitely molded, and looking at her evokes felicitous feelings. Yet this very quality tips the scales *against* Pulitzer's claim. Leonardo da Vinci's women are uniformly complex, mettlesome, self-assured. Portraits of haughty models such as Cecilia Gallerani, Isabella d'Este, Ginevra de' Benci— and of course the Gioconda—show people of considerable passion and human depth, willful at times, even imperious. By contrast, the Isleworth Lisa seems shallow, superficial, almost "too nice." In addition the background of this portrait is hasty and amateurish, totally unlike the craggy, otherworldly terrains favored by Leonardo.

In his stubborn war with the Louvre, Pulitzer fired a barrage of X-ray photos, densitometer tests and microchemical analyses, but none proved in the least conclusive. He also drafted an army of experts who came up with various theories, some of them contradictory. Commendatore Cecconi, curator of the Academy of Santa Luca, said, "For me, this is an original Leonardo." Dr. Cantalamesso of the Borghese Gallery theorized, "Undoubtedly from

Leonardo's studio, but I cannot give a further opinion."
Professor Fiocco of Venice said, "Definitely 'Leonardo
studio,'" but Dr. Anna Maria Brizio of Milan University
felt it came *after* the Louvre portrait and was "definitely
not Leonardo, but certainly Florentine." Professor Adolfo
Venturi thought Ambrogio da Predis was the principal
painter but agreed that it was "more beautiful than the
one in Paris." Dr. Colassanti, director of the Beaux-Arts,
felt that Melzi and not Leonardo had done most of the
work; and our old friend Professor Nicodemi "strongly
believed it to be French," attributing it to painter Jean
Perréal, who had lived in Paris in the 1500s.

Henry Pulitzer, who never wavered, died in March of
1979, a believer to the end. His former associate and
director for four years of the Pulitzer Gallery in London,
Teresa Van Wemmel, now lives in New York City. She
recalls, "He would get very discouraged at times and say
to me, 'It's hopeless—no one can discredit or question the
Louvre's *Mona Lisa*.' But he loved that painting and never
gave up his beliefs." Mrs. Van Wemmel, herself most
gracious and attractive, was impressed with her employer's
faith in his *Gioconda*. "He hung the picture in his drawing
room," she says, "and he practically lived in that room,
even had his meals there, just so he could be with the
Mona Lisa."

The Isleworth portrait came to America for a short
visit in 1962, was exhibited at the Galleries National in
Phoenix, Arizona, and during that time attracted much
local attention.

In the conclusion to his privately printed book
Pulitzer wrote: "I can only state again that even the most
wonderful of arguments and theories will not help to make
a painting more attractive or genuine. The *Mona Lisa* does
not really need propping up with arguments. This painting
speaks for itself to those who have eyes to see." Pulitzer's

Joconde is now in storage in Switzerland, awaiting disposition by the administrators of his estate.

The third and, in my view, by far the strongest claimant can be found in the United States, currently resting in a large plywood case in a bank vault in New Jersey. It also has the most colorful pedigree.

In 1797 an elegant American came home from France on a packet boat, bringing with him a number of fancy court costumes and some fifty valuable Old Masters, among them a Rembrandt, a Raphael, a Murillo and a Frans Hals. One of these paintings, listed on the inventory in his own script, was "A Nun—a finished picture by Leonardo da Vinci." William Henry Vernon had been sent abroad in 1778 after graduating from college, to learn the French language and acquire a bit of Old World polish. His father, William Vernon of Newport, Rhode Island, was a prominent shipbuilder, had been head of the Continental Navy Board during the American Revolution, and was a good friend of men such as Washington, Franklin, Adams and Lafayette. Unfortunately the elder Vernon's plans miscarried: young William took instantly to the life style of the French aristocracy, dressed himself as a courtier and became an intimate of dukes and princes, and the short sojourn abroad stretched out for almost twenty years. He also began to collect art with a fine, discriminating eye.

William Henry was imprisoned briefly during the French Revolution, later traveled to England and Russia, and finally, responding to pressures and pleas from home, returned to Newport with his brocaded finery and art masterpieces. Among these was the painting called "A Nun," which, according to family legend, had been given to William by none other than Marie Antoinette before her encounter with the guillotine in October 1793. One tale has it that the Queen of France gave the portrait to Vernon for safekeeping, hoping to reclaim it later; another says it was a gift to him for helping to save the life of her son, the Dauphin of France and heir to the throne.

In any event this duplicate of the Louvre's *Mona Lisa* was a special favorite of William's, cherished by him above all the others. When he died at the age of seventy-three his treasures were sold at auction, but the portrait ascribed to Leonardo was bought back for the Vernons and has been in the family ever since.

The reputation of this curious painting, and its publicity, have grown with the passing years. By coincidence, a few days before Perugia turned up in Florence with HIS *Mona Lisa,* a story appeared in *The New York Times* about the *Mona Lisa* of the Vernons. Poet Joyce Kilmer, then a young staff reporter, wrote: "The Vernon *Mona Lisa* is identical in expression with that [stolen] from the Louvre. Indeed, the paintings might easily be mistaken for each other." Kilmer closed with Walter Pater's classic description of the *Gioconda:* "Here is the head upon which all the ends of the world are come, and the eyelids are a little weary."

In 1929 William's "Nun" went to the Fogg Art Museum at Harvard University for cleaning and relining of the canvas; and according to the family, X-rays taken at the Fogg dated the canvas unmistakably from the da Vinci period. Further tests were later made by Dr. Thomas M. Judson of the American Academy in Rome and for many years a curator at the Vatican. Based on microscopic and infrared analyses Judson wrote, "The painting in my opinion is by the hand of Leonardo da Vinci." He referred to the fact that the master was lefthanded: "The brush strokes are *mano sinistra* throughout the painting," and added that this "bars attribution to any followers or pupils of Leonardo; the study of the X-ray shadowgraphs reveal Leonardo's technique in painting, which differs completely from that of his so-called school."

During those years the picture's champions were

Ambrose W. Vernon, a professor at Dartmouth, and his brother's widow, Alice C. E. Vernon. In one interview, feisty Mrs. Vernon was quoted as saying that she'd heard about some *Gioconda* forgeries being sold after the theft, but that "ours, of course, is the real thing." Other accounts appeared, including one in 1950 by Emily Genauer, art critic for the *New York Herald Tribune*, who reported:

> Neither of the Vernons suggests that the famous Louvre picture is not real. They merely submit that just as there are two versions by da Vinci of his famous canvas, "Madonna of the Rocks," one in the Louvre and one in London's National Gallery, so there are two versions of the "Mona Lisa."

In 1961, for its World Library series, Time-Life Books brought out a large, handsome volume on Italy; the section on Renaissance painting carried a print of the *Gioconda*, and under it: "Light and shadow frame the enigmatic smile of Leonardo da Vinci's *Mona Lisa*. The world's most famous portrait, it hangs in the Louvre in Paris." There was, however, a slight problem: the accompanying photograph didn't show the Louvre's *Mona Lisa* but the one owned by the Vernon family. ("Indeed," Joyce Kilmer had written in 1913, "the paintings might easily be mistaken for each other.") This piquant error was corrected in later editions of the book, but not before it had embarrassed a number of editors and gratified a number of Vernons.

Like the Pulitzer canvas, the Vernon madonna went west in 1964, to be successfully exhibited at the Otis Art Institute in Los Angeles. Then, after the death of Roger Vernon of New York City, it passed to a group of family heirs who now share joint ownership.

Alice Vernon's granddaughter Suzanne Vernon Swick, and her artist son Ford, accompanied me to a New Jersey bank for an audience with the controversial lady. This

Mona Lisa has always had a talent for drama, and the mood prevailed as it was carried out of the vault in its heavy wooden case, secured by assorted padlocks and metal bank seals. Mrs. Swick, personable and engaging, had seemed a bit defensive prior to our visit, as though anxious to protect a vulnerable family member. There was no need for her to be. The portrait, on emerging from its case, proved as captivating as it must have been to William Vernon almost two hundred years ago, when he hung it proudly on the wall of his Newport mansion. The colors are vibrant, the expression is lively and human, the background (unlike the others) is fully and subtly realized. Again, this *Joconde* appears younger than the lady in the Louvre.

The Vernon picture is on canvas, which was just then coming into use, especially in the ateliers of Venice. Almost all of da Vinci's paintings are oil on wood panels, but in a few cases, such as *The Virgin of the Rocks* and *Bacchus,* he did shift to a canvas surface, and there is no reason to rule out the possibility that he may have done so here. A close look under strong magnification also indicates that the brushwork, though muted, conforms to the directional cast of left-handed painters.

Miss Agnes Mongan, distinguished curator emerita of the Fogg Museum and an authority on da Vinci drawings, has clarified this. Right-handed artists, she explains, invariably add shading, toning or "crosshatching" on a slant pattern from the upper right to the lower left. Conversely, left-handed artists add hatching or shading which slants from upper left to lower right. "It's the natural way one's hand moves," she says. "It's almost impossible to draw any other way; try it for yourself and see." Miss Mongan referred to da Vinci's *mano sinistra:* "Leonardo painted left-handed, and it *is* possible to detect left-handed work. Or right-handed work, for that matter. X-rays of Rembrandt's paintings, for instance, show right-hand brush strokes. And it's possible to see left-handed painting with Bosch and Holbein the Younger."

Agnes Mongan finds no reason to question the Louvre's portrait—either its beauty or its credibility—nor would she offer any opinion as to the Vernon claims; but she does seem to feel that the question of brushwork is important. "I have never heard anyone in my fifty years in the trade," she says, "discuss the *Mona Lisa* from the standpoint of left-handed painting." The implications are that perhaps a useful clue is being neglected.

Today the Vernons are all, without exception, dedicated believers. "We have no quarrel with the Louvre," Mrs. Swick says, echoing her forebears. "We just feel that da Vinci painted two versions of the *Mona Lisa*—and ours is one of them."

The path of the Vernon challenger hasn't been entirely smooth. Some years ago, at the request of a trustee, the painting was evaluated by the International Foundation for Art Research. While these findings were confidential, the I.F.A.R. experts apparently took issue with Dr. Judson, stating that they felt the technical evidence was inconclusive. They theorized that the portrait was not by Leonardo, but was perhaps a seventeenth-century derivative of the original *Mona Lisa*.

This evaluation overlooks a number of key factors. If the Vernon lady were indeed a simple seventeenth-century copy of the Louvre portrait, why does the subject appear younger than in the original? Most copyists of masterpieces try hard to reproduce faces, colors and expressions as faithfully as possible. In view of this, why do *all three* of the contending portraits show a woman patently more youthful than the current occupant of the Grande Galerie? If they are derivative, from whom do they derive?

Then there's the riddle of the missing columns. Art historians all agree that at one time the *Mona Lisa* was

flanked by two architectural columns, the bases of which
are still slightly visible on the panel. A famous 1505 sketch
by Raphael based on the *Gioconda* (and also in the Louvre)
shows these pillars clearly. It is now believed that in the
mid-1500s, while the portrait was in Francis's royal baths
and before it became widely prominent, a few inches were
sliced from each side, probably to make it fit a particular
frame. If so, then how could the Vernon portrait, which
shows these columns, have been a copy made in the
seventeenth century, *long after* the original panel was
mutilated?

These flanking pillars do *not* appear on the Hekking
Joconde, and since we know that the columns weren't
cropped from the panel until sometime after it went to
King Francis, this negates the Hekkings' claim that their
portrait is by Leonardo. Henry Pulitzer's version does show
this feature, but as noted earlier, the background is
amateurish, and Lisa's bland, innocuous expression strongly
marks this as the work of a diligent copyist rather than of
the master. So only the Vernon entry seems to retain
credibility.

Beyond that, one big question finally remains to be
answered: is the *Mona Lisa* now in the Louvre a genuine
da Vinci, or is it a fake?

31

"To enjoy the *Mona Lisa*," Theodore Rousseau wrote,
"a man of the twentieth century must be capable of putting
out of his mind everything he has ever read about it." On
the contrary, in the realm of art what is read and learned
can clarify feelings and heighten perceptivity. Having seen
the Louvre portrait in earlier years, I returned to it many

times during the research for this book. Observation is cerebral as well as physical, and the effects of concentrated viewing were overwhelming: standing in front of this controversial painting, studying it now with more knowledgeable eyes, I felt clearly that I was in the presence of genius.

In my opinion the Louvre *Mona Lisa* is undeniably genuine, a true masterpiece of Leonardo's. Despite all the attacks, broadsides and verbal cannonading, this "certain Florentine lady" remains unshaken—scarred only by the normal attrition of time. If in fact this picture is a forgery, then there has existed somewhere an unknown, unsung artist whose consummate skill equaled that of one of the greatest minds in creative history.

The work is unsigned, but abounds in Leonardo's iconography. Lisa's smile appears (though less intensely) on other da Vinci faces, in *Lady with an Ermine,* the *Virgin and Child with Saint Anne* and the final painting, *Saint John the Baptist.* The splendid modeling of her hands, the pose of her figure are pure da Vinci and have been imitated by masters such as Raphael, Joos van Cleve and Jean-Baptiste Corot.

The background, more moonscape than Tuscan countryside, can be found again in Leonardo's *Virgin of the Rocks* and *Madonna with the Carnation.* His *sfumato* technique—a misty blending of light and shade to create solid form without sharp outlines—is powerfully evident in *La Joconde.* Da Vinci's left-handed brushwork is also visible, particularly in the mountain peaks beyond the sitter's face, and this *substantially disqualifies* the apprentices then working in the master's studio.

When the picture came back to Paris in January of 1914, it was checked carefully by France's leading art experts, and according to Émile Bollaërt they "knew *La Joconde* well, and all recognized her." The authorities who examined the portrait were Léon Bonnat, Raymond

Kochlin, Charles Bénoist, Étienne Dinet, Joseph Reinach and Henri Marcel; also MM. Pujalet, Jacquier, Cottin, Bomier, Paul-Léon, Bénédite and Leprieur. It defies reason to suppose that *all* of these men were fooled—not even Chaudron could have accomplished that. On file at the Louvre are X rays and photos of the *Mona Lisa* going back to 1900, and some show specific markings and *craquelure* patterns in detail. These could easily have been compared with Perugia's panel, inch by inch, and a fake would have been quickly unmasked.

What if the group knowingly authenticated a forgery in order to save face for the Louvre? Again, it is hardly conceivable that these authorities—the cream of the French art world—could all have plotted to trick the public and accept a substitution. Surely some of them would have rejected and denounced the scheme; after all, there had been other false alarms in the hunt for *La Joconde,* and one more could hardly have mattered. In short, there's absolutely no factual basis for assuming a secret Louvre plot. Conspiracy theories have their appeal, but also their limits in logic.

Renaissance scholar Walter Pater wrote of the *Mona Lisa,* "Set it for a moment beside one of those white Greek goddesses or beautiful women of antiquity, and how they would be troubled by this beauty, into which the soul with all its maladies has passed!" The painting breathes conviction, and in time I came to agree with Madeleine Hours: I had seen numerous versions, but never found any (with one exception, to be discussed) which matched the Louvre's lady for craftsmanship and beauty. The sheer authority of technique and nuances of expression stamp this as a Vincian masterwork.

However, the story doesn't end here, since other mysteries must be solved. Why does Vasari say that Leonardo painted Donna Lisa for Signore del Giocondo, while Antonio de Beatis, a scrupulous secretary, tells us clearly that this Florentine lady was painted "from life, at the request of the late Magnificent, Giuliano de' Medici"? And if da Vinci began Lisa's portrait in 1503—or even earlier—why did he keep it with him, supposedly unfinished, until his death in 1519? Leonardo was a procrastinator who often neglected his art to pursue experiments in science, astronomy and military engineering, but even for him a sixteen-year span is excessive. Besides, having returned from Milan empty-handed, he was short of funds and would have jumped at the chance to finish this simple project and collect his fee.

But let's set this aside and agree that, for some reason, he did keep Lisa's picture with him until the end. Why, then, did it go to the French King instead of to the man who commissioned it? And why, during his last years at Cloux, did Leonardo show Lisa's portrait (it could have been no other) to Cardinal Louis and his secretary, telling them it had been created for his Medici ex-patron? This same panel was listed in King Francis's records as "A courtesan with a gauze veil," as if to somehow hide its identity. Another mystery concerns the gap in age between the Louvre's *Joconde* and other versions. Not all of these show a younger woman, but a significant number do, indicating that some copyists worked from *a different painting*.

There are, of course, as many theories about the *Mona Lisa* as there are historians who have analyzed her. But gaps and discrepancies continue to baffle the experts. Having lived with this lady for some years, during which scores of books, essays, documents, records and other data were explored—and having talked with many people whose knowledge far exceeds my own—I began to fit various forgotten pieces of the puzzle into place. Arriving at an answer from these tantalizing evidential bits was like reconstructing the skull of Pithecanthropus man from a fragment of jawbone, but a coherent and logical picture gradually emerged and can now be presented.

It's my conviction that during his lifetime Leonardo did paint TWO *Mona Lisa*s. The second and more prestigious of these is the familiar belle of Paris. Her obscure younger sister, the original version, is reposing in a vault in New Jersey. It was quite customary for masters of that era to paint more than one copy of a favorite subject. Leonardo himself did two versions in his youth of the *Annunciation,* one currently in the Uffizi Gallery and the other in the Louvre. Later he painted nearly identical versions of the famous *Virgin of the Rocks.* One of these is in the Louvre collection, the other in London's National Gallery. There are twin versions of *La Belle Ferronière;* also of *Leda and the Swan,* attributed to the school of Leonardo. Why not, then, two *Gioconda*s?

The existence of these portraits, *both from the brush of da Vinci,* clears up many contradictions, as will be seen.

In 1502 or 1503, Leonardo accepted a commission from Signore del Giocondo, a wealthy cloth manufacturer, to create a portrait of his handsome young wife. Donna Lisa had been born the daughter of Antonio di Noldo Gherardini, a prominent Florentine whose family was distantly related to the powerful Medici clan. There is evidence that as a girl Lisa Gherardini was a close friend of young Giuliano de' Medici, who appears on the scene later.

Before this commission, in March 1500, da Vinci had spent time in Venice, where he learned more about the use of linen canvas, a painting surface growing in popularity among Venetians. "Leonardo," writes Professor Max Doerner, "was devoted to technical experimentation, particularly in oils." The artist's curiosity was boundless; he constantly tried new methods of mixing colors, new ways of applying pigment to wood or plaster. He would also have been intrigued with this new use of canvas; and back in Florence, ready to begin Lisa's portrait, what better time to try it? The project wasn't too important, he could experiment with it safely—even use the results if he chose as a preliminary study for a later work.

But given Leonardo's gift for delay, even this simple picture took him three or four years to complete. When he began working on details of the face and figure, Lisa came regularly to the studio to pose, and the two became good friends. Vasari reports: "Leonardo also made use of this device: while he was painting Mona Lisa, who was a very beautiful woman, he employed singers and musicians or jesters to keep her full of merriment and so chase away the melancholy that painters usually give to portraits." It should be added that students and apprentices joined in these painting sessions, studying Leonardo's methods and attempting their own copies and sketches. Some of these disciples were extremely talented, and their work would later be of help.

Lisa One is in my belief the superb portrait now owned by William Vernon's descendants—a picture whose fragile canvas was carefully restored by the conservators of Harvard's Fogg Art Museum. Many aspects of the portrait fit Vasari's words: here are the soft flesh tones, rosy lips, delicate nostrils which he described so precisely. This Lisa also appears six or eight years younger than her sibling in the Louvre. Her face is a bit slimmer, her smile less jaded, and we can well imagine her reacting to the antics of da Vinci's singers and jesters. The columns of the loggia are there, as they once were on the Louvre painting, and the background is unquestionably Leonardesque, even to the *mano sinistra*.

While studying *Lisa One*, I realized that this was the first time she had ever sat for her portrait. It would ob- viously have been a rich and exciting experience for the young woman, and in her expression we find pleasure, vanity and a dash of pride at posing for so distinguished a painter. Seen at close hand, in its still-vibrant colors, the portrait creates a powerful impact; it glows with its own vitality, and the Vincian technique is impressive.

Establishing provenance after so many years is a tricky matter, but the accretion of evidence adds up to a persuasive case. And there are other supporting clues. McMullen mentions one theory which claims that "at some stage in the long process of her creation Leonardo intended her as a religious personage." This is based on the "somewhat saintly effect" caused by Lisa's loosely flowing hair, simple dress and complete lack of jewelry or ornaments, and by the fine mantle or veil over her head. So it's no accident that when William Vernon came home to America, his painting was entered on the bill of lading as "A Nun —a finished picture by Leonardo da Vinci." In Marie Antoinette's circle the portrait was fully accepted as genuine. Some of the pictures William brought back were listed "Artist unknown," but in this case the attribution was very clear.

Thomas Judson, who authenticated the Vernon *Gioconda,* also spoke of a "two *Mona Lisa*" theory. He wondered if the first portrait might perhaps have been interrupted by Lisa's ill health. Some years later, according to Judson, she may have returned to the artist's studio, and Leonardo, unwilling to rework the early portrait, decided to create a whole new version. This *Lisa* also won support from Francis Henry Taylor, who in the 1940s was the dynamic director of the Metropolitan Museum of Art. In a letter to a friend of the Vernon family he wrote, "I remember very well seeing the *Vernon Leonardo* at your home . . ." The emphasis is mine, the attribution Taylor's. Since he was a brilliant art curator who chose words with care, his precise reference to a *Leonardo* must be given substantial weight.

We can assume that after da Vinci completed this picture, probably late in 1507, it was delivered to Lisa's

patient husband, who hung it on the wall of his large villa
on the Via Stufa. (The Giocondo mansion, by odd coincidence, was located just a stone's throw from the Via
Panzani, where Vincenzo Perugia stayed when he arrived
in Florence so many decades later.)

The artist, meanwhile, went on to other projects.
Then, "in the summer of 1508," Kenneth Clark writes,
"Leonardo returned to Milan, which was to be his headquarters for the next five years." During that era the
Medici family, traditional rulers of Florence, had been
driven into exile, and power fell into the hands of the
fanatic monk Girolamo Savonarola. This zealot was
finally deposed and executed, and for some years the city
was ruled by a succession of petty despots. Then in 1512,
backed by a strong Spanish army, the Medicis returned
and took control again amid general rejoicing. Da Vinci,
a favorite of the Medici clan, also came back to his beloved
city.

The following year Giuliano de' Medici, whose brother
had become Pope Leo X, was appointed ruler of Florence.
Giuliano was a chivalrous, courtly, handsome addition to
Florentine society. He had a variety of mistresses, and soon
after his return to the sumptuous Palazzo Medici on the
Via Cavour still another noblewoman caught his eye. Some
months later he commissioned Leonardo to do a portrait
of this new paramour—none other than his childhood
friend, Lisa del Giocondo. This is of course the celebrated
painting now in the Louvre, which was snatched from the
Carré in 1911.

So in effect the Vernon portrait became a preliminary
model for *Lisa Two,* which shows the master at the height
of his powers. This also explains the endless confusion
about the picture being unfinished. Casual visitors to the
studio who vaguely remembered the earlier version could
easily have been misled, and might naturally assume—
given Leonardo's reputation—that he was indeed *still work-*

ing on the original portrait. Though he tried canvas at times, da Vinci preferred the traditional poplar surface, and this was again used for his second *Mona Lisa.*

Leonardo loved pranks and had a great reputation as a practical joker. He was an irreverent man, unimpressed by the rich (though he welcomed their commissions), and equally casual with nobles and commoners. So it's entirely consistent with his nature that in 1513 he should carry out a fine aesthetic jest: the design of the first portrait had pleased him and had proven very successful, so he chose to paint Lisa for her powerful lover in the exact same pose he had used for her aging husband. And perhaps here at last, we have an explanation for the derisive *Gioconda* smile.

Another possibility is that when he returned to Florence, de' Medici saw the original, admired it greatly, and specifically *ordered* a similar version for himself. Since there were numerous studies made earlier by art students —including the famous sketch by Raphael in 1505—and since the first portrait was still available on the Via Stufa, it would have been simple enough for a master like da Vinci to recapture and duplicate the pose, the colors, the background.

The two *Mona Lisa*s are uncannily alike—but the second does show subtle differences. This is decidedly not the fresh, youthful woman described so eloquently by Vasari. Much has happened over the years; now her look is more cynical, and in Pater's words the eyelids are "a little weary." Lisa's face, befitting a woman in her thirties, is fuller than in the first study, and there are hints of an incipient double chin. Both artist and subject had matured, and this eloquent painting—typical of later works—shows the master at his best, the modeling and *sfumato* technique eloquently realized.

We can deduce that *Lisa Two* was finished—or almost finished—by 1515; but then an unexpected hitch developed. Historian G. F. Young writes that in that year Giuliano de' Medici was sent as an envoy of Pope Leo X to congratulate the new King of France, Francis I; and "while at the French court Giuliano was married to the charming Philiberte of Savoy, then seventeen years old." Giuliano was the soul of tact, and with a new bride coming home to his palace it would hardly do to have a portrait of his favorite mistress staring at her from the wall. So Leonardo was quietly paid for his work and instructed to keep the painting in his studio for the time being.

Now the final pieces of the puzzle fall into place. Giuliano de' Medici was sickly (it's believed that he was tubercular), and in March of 1516, a short year after his marriage to Philiberte, he died. Today his tomb, designed by Michelangelo, can be seen in the ancient Church of San Lorenzo in Florence. The following year Leonardo, still faithfully guarding *Lisa Two,* went to Amboise and settled in the Château of Cloux as a guest of King Francis. Here he stayed for the last years of his life, and when Leonardo died in 1519 the *Mona Lisa* passed into the King's collection. There is some confusion as to how he acquired it—whether it was a gift or a sale, or even why he was made the recipient. Although the fact has been generally overlooked, Leonardo had a very valid reason. The late Giuliano de' Medici's wife, Philiberte, was the younger sister of Francis's mother, Louise of Savoy. So she was the King's aunt, and what better way to dispose of Giuliano's incriminating picture—his mysterious "Florentine lady"— than to leave it to the kind monarch *who was de' Medici's nephew*?

The tidy balance of this would have appealed to the aged artist, and it further explains why, for reasons of tact and family politics, the portrait was left unidentified in the King's catalogue.

Now a final question remains: how did the original *Mona Lisa* get from the household of Francesco del

Giocondo to the hands so many years later of Marie
Antoinette, who in turn presented it to William Henry
Vernon? Here there are no records or documents, and we
are obliged to speculate.

Italy in the fifteenth and sixteenth centuries was
plagued by endless wars between the independent city-
states—Naples, Pisa, Rome, Milan—as well as invasions
by mercenary armies crossing the Alps from Spain, France
and Germany. The wealthy Florentines managed to escape
destruction by clever political maneuvering, plus the payment of huge ransoms; but in 1530, attacked by a powerful
army under the Hapsburg Emperor Charles V, they decided to resist. After ten months of courageous fighting, the
defending forces were overcome and the mercenaries swept
into the city to loot and plunder. It is possible that before this the *Mona Lisa*, along with other treasures, was
smuggled out of beseiged Florence and sent to France for
safekeeping. More likely, it was carried off as part of the
spoils of war, in the baggage train of some victorious
European nobleman.

In those centuries, valuable works of art such as
paintings, sculpture, rich tapestries and fine silver plate
were often used as a kind of bribe, presented by aspiring
courtiers to powerful dukes and princes in return for favors
granted. *Lisa One,* this splendid portrait of Leonardo's,
could easily have made her way over the decades from one
ducal palace to another, coming at last into the hands of
that expert and tireless favor-granter, the daughter of Maria
Theresa of Austria and wife of Louis XVI of France. From
her keeping, as we now know, the portrait passed to William
Vernon, who brought it with him to America, where it has
remained ever since.

This, then, is in my opinion the story of the two *Mona
Lisa*s and how Leonardo came to paint them. The presenta-
tion fits all the available historic data and helps to clear up

numerous paradoxes. Many pieces of the *Gioconda* puzzle
now fit. But not all of them. Lisa and the man who im-
mortalized her are and always will be creatures of endless
depth and nuance. The sphinx and her sorcerer stub-
bornly resist easy comprehension. Perhaps this is what
prompted McMullen to state that "the *Mona Lisa,* along
with many of the masterpieces in all the arts, must finally
be interpreted as simply an eloquent question." And,
echoing this, Clark writes in his classic study, "Leonardo is
the Hamlet of art history whom each of us must recreate
for himself."

32

TODAY THEY STREAM by the thousands through the Porte
Denon into the Musée du Louvre, and officials estimate
that nearly three million people now visit every year, many
of them eager for a close look at the museum's star attraction and her noted smile.

The expression of the *Gioconda* has been called everything from sly to sublime, enticing to repellent. Michelangelo thought the smile "divinely ironic"; it has also been
termed sensual, cynical, inviting, asthmatic, witty, seduc-
tive, tender, scornful, eerie, remote, voluptuous, magnetic,
all-knowing and ice-cold. Vasari referred to the portrait as
"a thing more divine than human." Théophile Gautier
said, "One feels like a schoolboy before a duchess." Pater
thought of it as da Vinci's "ideal lady, embodied and be-
held at last," and painter Odilon Redon called her face "a
human visage with the radiance of pure spirit." In the
opposite camp, Paul Valéry dismissed the smile as "a mere
wrinkle on a countenance." Noted critic Bernard Berenson,
at first an enthusiast, changed his mind and rejected the
portrait: "What I really saw . . . was the estranging image

of a woman beyond the reach of my sympathies," adding
that she had an "air of hostile superiority." And Dr. Freud,
ever the clinician, called it simply "the lost smile of
Leonardo's mother."

This much analyzed panel, after returning from Italy,
had other adventures. In 1914, with the armies of General
von Moltke menacing Paris, the *Mona Lisa* was hastily
evacuated to Bordeaux; and after the armistice it went
back to the Louvre. At the outbreak of World War II
it was again crated and, with other treasures, was moved
for safekeeping to Chambord, then to a basement in the
Château de Chévigny, east of Poitiers. Later the madonna
returned to Paris and remained there until her historic
seven-week trip in 1963 to the United States, where an
estimated 1.6 million visitors paid court to her in Washington, D.C., and New York City. The picture made
another long journey in 1974, going to the National
Museum in Tokyo, then to the Pushkin Museum in
Moscow. In those countries additional millions saw
the masterpiece, including Communist official Leonid
Brezhnev, who purportedly glanced at it and said, "A
plain, sensible-looking woman."

Today the *Mona Lisa* is no longer in the Salon Carré
but in a large bay off the main Picture Gallery called the
Salle des États, where it hangs in a specially built alcove,
humidity-regulated, temperature-controlled, electronically
guarded, and shielded by bullet-proof glass. During visiting hours there is always a large cluster of pilgrims milling
about in front of the exhibit as before a shrine; these
viewers stare at the painting intently with varying degrees
of wonder and curiosity, also disappointment ("I never
realized it was so *small*"). For most newcomers to the
Louvre, seeing the *Gioconda* is a major experience; yet it's
unlikely that many know the unique story behind the picture—a chronology of theft, forgery, secret sales, fumbling

investigators, machinations, and challenges to its veracity. Nor are they aware that she has a younger sister living in obscurity on the other side of the Atlantic.

Very little has altered physically at the Louvre since that crucial August day in 1911. The storeroom off the Salle Duchatel, where Perugia and the Lancelottis hid overnight, is still there behind its *trompe l'oeil* door; but artists' supplies are now kept elsewhere and the Duchatel alcove is used for storing electrical and lighting equipment. It is also possible to retrace most of the route taken by the gang on Monday morning when they carried *La Joconde* out of the Carré, across the Grande Galerie, down the service stairway and out through the Visconti Gate.

Perhaps the chief difference is that, unlike those earlier casual days, there are guards everywhere and the populous salons and galleries are now crawling with security men equipped with the latest detection and surveillance devices.

The museum setting remains largely unchanged, but of the principals in the drama only the *Mona Lisa* and the doubts survive.

Louis Beroud, the Lancelotti brothers, Françoise Séguenot, Mathilde, Jack Dean and other minor players faded away, and nothing is known of their later years. The forger Chaudron continued as before to live quietly in a comfortable manor house south of Paris; after the great swindle he retired more or less permanently, though on occasion, according to the Marqués, he took on a "special assignment." Why do we know so little about this artist and his frauds, and how is it he was never publicly unmasked? The answer is as simple as it is obvious: because he was successful. Unlike notorious forgers such as Alceo Dossena, Hans van Meegeren, Elmyr de Hory and Henri Haddad ("David Stein"), all of whose careers have been publicized, Yves Chaudron never overreached himself; instead he preserved his cover, his craft and not incidentally his freedom by avoiding the usual ego pitfalls. "The forger," Jeppson pointed out, "is an adventurer," and most adventurers are prone to take risks. But Chaudron had a talent for caution as well as art, and managed to cover himself effectively at all times. He was also a brilliant craftsman whose facsimiles were authentic and convincing, bringing to mind a comment by Theodore Rousseau. At a Metropolitan Museum seminar in 1967, speaking of art counterfeiters, he said, "We should all realize that we can only talk about the bad forgeries, the ones that have been detected; the good ones are still hanging on the walls."

The forger's mentor Eduardo de Valfierno, who had been ailing for some years, died in 1931 not long after his final meeting with his friend Decker; and his body was returned to Buenos Aires for interment. The Marqués had always been something of a black sheep, but it isn't likely that any of the distinguished, solemn-faced relatives attending his burial ceremony had the slightest idea that this member of their aristocratic family had masterminded the wildest art theft of the century. Decker published a short account of the caper after the Marqués's death, but it failed to create much stir at that time in Depression-ridden America.

As for Vincenzo Perugia, he returned to Dumenza shortly after his release and was welcomed home as a hero by his family, the mayor, the local townspeople and most of Lombardy. The country was then at war and Perugia joined the Italian Army, where he served honorably until the conflict ended. In 1921 he married a second cousin and tried, without success, to find adequate work in Italy. Ironically, despite his professed Francophobia, Vincenzo then went back to France with his new wife and opened a paint-and-varnish store in Haute-Savoie, near Geneva. Here the Perugias apparently did well and lived quietly; and in September of 1947 at the age of sixty-six, in the town of Annemasse, the *Gioconda*'s abductor finally died. This event passed largely unnoticed, but a local journalist reported that it had been for love of a woman who was "a true reincarnation of the *Mona Lisa*" that Perugia had stolen the painting. "But his passion was not cured," the reporter went on, "and it was the name of the *Mona Lisa* that he murmured still as he breathed his last."

In the city of Florence on the Via Panzani, wearing a bright awning of coral and white, stands the tiny Hotel La Gioconda, formerly the Tripoli-Italia. Though still a modest inn, it is today far more inviting than it was in pre-Perugia years, the theft and publicity having imparted a certain panache. The hotel is prosperous, the small lobby neat and attractive, and the present concierge, Signore Giovanni Chiabra, is only too happy to regale visitors with the story of the famous crime.

Chiabra has many of his facts wrong but makes up for it with his enthusiasm, and is quick to press into one's hands a brochure which carries a photograph of the *Mona Lisa* plus a legend in Italian, French, English and German:

In this hotel in 1913
was recovered LA GIOCONDA
stolen from the Louvre.

Hanging high above the desk where "Vincenzo Leonard" once signed the shabby register is a full-sized replica of the *Mona Lisa*. Chiabra points to this with pride. "A copy made in 1933," he says in careful English. "Painted on a glass pane. Very excellent. Made by a very fine artist."

The glass madonna, sensitively portrayed, glitters as she gazes down at the lobby where her prototype arrived years ago in the bottom of a small wooden trunk. As the concierge notes, it's an excellent copy, yet something in the expression is unsettling; unlike the Louvre's *Mona Lisa,* this lady is a shade too merry, her grin just a little too broad. She stares at the viewer boldly, her smile verging on the irrepressible, as if at any moment she may burst out to reveal an absurd secret.

Notes and Sources

PART ONE: The Robbery

PAGE

18: Paris, that summer of 1911 . . . *et seq.* For this and subsequent data on Paris life in the early 1900s I am indebted to *Paris au jour le jour* by Elizabeth Hausser (Paris: Éditions de Minuit, 1968). Other helpful sources were *La Belle Époque*, edited by Enzo Orlandi and Lorenzo Camusso (New York: William Morrow, 1978); *Paris Was Yesterday*, by Janet Flanner (New York: Viking Press, 1968); *The Good Years*, by Walter Lord (New York: Harper & Row, 1960); and the U.S. and French newspaper files of the period.

20: . . . a picture was missing . . . *et seq.* Beroud's discovery touched off the crime story of the decade. The *Mona Lisa* was really the first great masterpiece to be so brazenly—and successfully—lifted, but today such crimes have reached epidemic levels. Law enforcers now estimate that $100 million worth of art and antiques is stolen annually in Europe and the United States, and during the past five years some 28,000 paintings disappeared in Italy alone.

Though security systems have improved vastly, no institution is immune. In recent years the Louvre has been joined by noted victims such as New York's Metropolitan Museum, Boston's Museum of Fine Arts, the Philadelphia Museum of Art, the Fine Arts Museum of San Francisco, Chicago's Art Institute, the Fine Arts Museum in Düsseldorf, the Berlin National Gallery, the Stedlijk in Amsterdam, Leningrad's Hermitage, Knoedler's in Paris, Milan's Galleria Moderna, the Montreal Museum of Fine Arts, the Hamburg Museum, and the Museum of Modern Art in Barcelona. Scores of churches, public art centers, auction houses, commercial galleries, private mansions and archaeological sites have also been plundered. With today's easy access to markets all over the world, fine art has thus become a tangible and highly desirable form of investment. In addition, artwork is nonreplenishing. No

matter how prolific, every painter, every sculptor can produce only
so much in a lifetime—and with the law of supply and demand
operating at full force, prices inevitably skyrocket.

Society now offers plenty of motivation for its art thieves, but
the 1911 Louvre caper still remains the granddaddy of museum
burglaries. At the time it was a scandal without parallel; Paris
newspapers devoted endless pages to the story, and scores of articles
appeared in magazines and periodicals. The coverage gradually
faded, then exploded once again when Perugia brought the missing
portrait to Florence.

Surprisingly little of this fascinating material has ever been
collated and compiled. A very good if brief account of the theft
and recovery can be found in Milton Esterow's *The Art Stealers*
(see below). Esterow, editor/publisher of *ARTnews* and *Antiques
World,* detailed some but not all of the main highlights. Other
references to the crime, appearing in various histories, consist of
a page or two at most or a few brief paragraphs. But to my knowledge, no fully comprehensive account of this caper and its perpe-
trators has appeared in print until now.

24:   "It is not enough to say . . ." From the introduction by Milton
S. Fox to *Art Treasures of the Louvre,* by René Huyghe (New York:
H. N. Abrams, 1951), p. 9. Other background information on the
museum is from *The Louvre,* by Germaine Bazin (Abrams, 1958);
The Louvre, by Konody and Rockwell (London: T. C. Jack, 1910);
Karl Baedeker's classic guide, *Paris and Its Environs* (London:
T. F. Unwin, 1907); and *Le Louvre* (Paris: Éditions des Musées
Nationaux, 1977).

32:   ". . . the mode to have taste." *The Proud Possessors,* by Aline B.
Saarinen (New York: Random House, 1958), introduction, p. xx.

32:   ". . . countries of origin." Essays by E. H. Roditi, *Encyclopaedia
Britannica* (1966), Vol. II, p. 514.

33:   "a pale wisp of a Frenchman . . ." "Why and How the Mona
Lisa Was Stolen," by Karl Decker, *Saturday Evening Post,* June
25, 1932, p. 15.

33:   "Chaudron and I . . ." *Ibid.,* p. 15.

40:   ". . . it's worth millions." *The Art Stealers,* by Milton Esterow
(New York: Macmillan, 1973), p. 113.

On the general subject of art theft, other helpful sources were
The Plundered Past, by Karl E. Meyer (New York: Atheneum,
1977), and *The Art Crisis,* by Bonnie Burnham (New York: St.
Martin's, 1975). An additional valuable source was a privately
circulated report of the I.F.A.R., prepared in 1978 by Mrs.

Burnham, *Art Theft: Its scope, its impact, its control.* Periodicals in recent years have carried many articles on this subject. Among these are "Danger: Art Thieves!," *Life* magazine, March 1979; "Culture Vultures," by Bonnie Burnham, *Saturday Review,* Sept. 1, 1979; "Smuggled!," by Bryan Rostron, *Saturday Review,* March 31, 1979; and "Artful Thieves," by Pranay Gupte, *New York Times Magazine,* July 22, 1979.

PART TWO: The Ruse

PAGE

52: It was essential for a startled world . . . "Why and How the Mona Lisa Was Stolen," by Karl Decker, *Saturday Evening Post,* June 25, 1932. Of all successful art swindles, Valfierno's ruse remains in a class by itself. Journalist Decker's account first appeared in 1932. Later the story was retold (briefly) in two books, both of which substantiated the basic facts and added certain new details and background material. These sources are *Lock, Stock and Barrel,* by Douglas and Elizabeth Rigby (Philadelphia: Lippincott, 1944); and *The Fabulous Frauds,* by Lawrence Jeppson (New York: Weybright and Talley, 1970). The forgery scheme was referred to in *Hoaxes,* by Curtis D. MacDougall (New York: Dover, 1940); *Art Fakes in America,* by David L. Goodrich (New York: Viking, 1973); and a number of feature articles in the 1930s. Goodrich also quotes, (p. 142), the prominent art dealer Joseph Duveen to the effect that many copies have been made of Leonardo's works "and offered in the market as genuine."

Some years after this, in 1955, the Paris Prefecture sponsored its Salon des Faux, organized by Commissioner Isnard, in which a number of *Mona Lisa* forgeries were exhibited—but the police never disclosed the pedigrees of these.

54: In the old days . . . *et seq.* Decker, *op. cit.,* p. 89. The man behind the *Gioconda* ruse, "Eduardo de Valfierno," remains an exasperatingly shadowy figure in this narrative. Even as careful a historian as Jeppson concedes in the epilogue to his account (*op. cit.,* p. 318) that the swindler ". . . defies positive verification." Nonetheless, circumstantial evidence on the elusive Marqués is abundant and is backed by supportive facts. Karl Decker, the man to whom Valfierno confided, died in New York City in 1941, leaving his wife, Maud, but no other survivors; and a lengthy obituary in *The New York Times* (Dec. 5, 1941) detailed his eminent career as a journalist. For most of his professional years Decker was with the Hearst organization and also served as chief of the Washington bureau of the Universal News Service. He was an adventurous and enterprising reporter, cast in the mold of Richard Harding Davis and the young Hemingway; in his travels he met many of the flamboyant boulevardiers and raffish *bon vivants* of his era, and it is logical that he would have numbered the Marqués among them.

55: ". . . hidden in a corner." Jeppson, *op. cit.,* p. 32.

58: ". . . there will be forgeries." From "Art and Authenticity," by Frank Jewell Mather, *Atlantic Monthly,* March 1929, p. 310.

60: "The potential forger . . ." *Ibid.,* p. 311.

60: ". . . work by an unknown." *The Art of the Faker,* by Frank Arnau (Boston: Little, Brown, 1961), p. 10.

60: The shadowy Yves Chaudron . . . *et seq.* Decker, *op. cit.* Like Valfierno, Chaudron eludes clear identification. However, Isnard and other experts have referred in their writings to a legendary art forger, supposedly more brilliant—and more successful—than any of those ever caught by the authorities. This mystery man, who was never named by them, may well have been the Marqués's self-effacing copyist from Marseilles.

68: ". . . susceptible to corruption." Jeppson, *op. cit.,* p. 31. A distinction must be made between, on the one hand, innocent dupes who buy fakes under the impression that they are legitimate works by prominent painters and, on the other, venal collectors who obtain forgeries believing them to be masterpieces stolen from a particular museum, church or archaeological site.

The Marqués's clients belonged, of course, to the latter category, but many astute curators and collectors have been innocently saddled with frauds. Pierpont Morgan, mentioned several times in these pages, once bought a portrait by Ridolfo Ghirlandajo which had been retouched and sold to him as a genuine Raphael. On another occasion he acquired a jeweled book cover by Benvenuto Cellini which turned out later to be a 19th-century German forgery. Other wealthy collectors who were periodically victimized include Cornelius Vanderbilt, Walter P. Chrysler and the financier August Belmont. During those years money, naïveté and a thirst for status led to a great tidal wave of frauds flooding into the United States. An oft-quoted joke in art circles says that of the 2,000 paintings made by Corot in his lifetime 5,000 can be found in American collections. And in 1927 artist George Luks, while helping to set

up an exhibit at the Carnegie Art Galleries in Pittsburgh, stormed
to reporters (*New York Times,* Jan. 31, 1927), "Fifty percent of
the 'old masters' in the collections of Pittsburgh's millionaires are
fake!" They had all been, he insisted, hoaxed by "smooth and
ingenious" swindlers.

This ingenuity still persists. In 1967, while director of the Metropolitan Museum of Art, Thomas Hoving said, "Today forgers
seem to be all around us, and indeed there's a cleverness now, an
acuteness that often defies description."

68:   ". . . preparing them mentally." Decker, *op. cit.,* p. 89.

68:   "Imagine the hours . . ." *et seq. The Only Way to Cross,* by
John Maxtone-Graham (New York: Collier Books, 1972), p. 209.

69:   The psychologist Dr. Henry Codet . . . *et seq.* This and other
information on the collecting obsession is from *The Great Collectors,* by Pierre Cabanne (New York: Farrar, Straus, 1963).

69;   ". . . to trust them." *Ibid.,* preface, p. x.

70:   After some intense weeks . . . Decker, *op. cit.,* p. 91.

The literature of art forgery is extensive. In addition to Frank
Arnau's invaluable book (*op. cit.*), useful sources were *Forgers,
Dealers, Experts,* by Sepp Schüller (New York: G. P. Putnam's
Sons, 1960); *The Art Game,* by Robert Wraight (New York: Simon
and Schuster, 1965); *Faux et imitations dans l'art,* by Guy Isnard
(Paris: Librairie Arthème Fayard, 1959); a folio, *Art Forgery,*
published by the Metropolitan Museum of Art (Bulletin No. 6,
February 1968); and the writings of Dr. Sheldon Keck.

Magazine and feature stories include "Art and Authenticity," by
Frank J. Mather, *Atlantic Monthly,* March 1929; "The Gentle Art
of Faking," by Alfred Frankfurter, *ARTnews,* February 1954;
"Fakes and Frauds in the Art World," by Ralph Colin, *Art in
America,* April 1963; and "On Fakes, Frauds and Forgeries," by
Hilton Kramer, *New York Times,* Jan. 7, 1968.

PART THREE: The Reaction

PAGE

75:   On black Tuesday . . . *et seq.* Most of the material for this
section came from accounts in the European and American press,
particularly the French newspapers of 1911—and for these I was
generously given access to the files of the Paris Prefecture of Police
and the Louvre's Dept. of Documentation. Supplementary details

came from later news reports plus recapitulations of the crime after the painting was recovered, and all such sources and dates are cited in the body of the text. Other data is from *The Art Stealers,* by Milton Esterow (New York: Macmillan, 1973); *Mona Lisa, the Picture and the Myth,* by Roy McMullen (Boston: Houghton Mifflin, 1975), and from personal interviews noted. In developing the social and historic background of these events, McMullen's graceful account has proved most helpful.

76: ". . . try to steal it." Picquet's comment reported by Esterow, *op. cit.,* p. 114.

77: *"La Joconde* is gone. . . ." *Ibid.,* p. 112.

79: Comment in *Le Figaro. Ibid.,* p. 117.

84: The Prefecture then appealed . . . *et seq. Ibid.,* p. 124.

85: . . . a letter-cum-memoir . . . *et. seq.,* Campbell's letter, dated Feb. 16, 1963, came to light during my research at the Louvre in June 1979.

88: Among those on record . . . The spiritualists' predictions were covered regularly in the French press and were summed up in a survey in *Le Figaro* on Sept. 4, 1911.

92: ". . . possessed only a copy." Esterow (*op. cit.,* p. 120) quotes Reinach's theory.

92: "humor, faddism and hucksterism." McMullen, *op. cit.,* p. 205.

94: ". . . discredit each other." This and other references to the shortcomings of the French police system are from *Secrets of the Sûreté,* by Jean Belin (New York: G. P. Putnam's Sons, 1950), p. 127.

96: But as Sauvet explained . . . *et seq.* Since the plumber was the chief evidentiary link between Perugia and the Lancelotti brothers, it is worth noting again that at the time he encountered them in the stairwell he had no idea whatever (nor did anyone else) that the *Mona Lisa* had been stolen. None of the men had distinctive features, and in the dim light Sauvet barely glanced at them. So he was quite unable to describe them adequately to the police during subsequent questioning.

98: Picasso's anxious partner . . . *et seq.* Pablo Picasso's involvement in the robbery's aftermath is well documented but, surprisingly, not widely known. Accounts and details vary, but many reliable facts can be found in *Picasso and His Friends* (New York: Appleton-Century, 1965), by Picasso's onetime mistress Fernande Olivier. Other sources were *Picasso,* by Antonina Vallentin (New York: Doubleday, 1963); *The Banquet Years,* by Roger Shattuck

(New York: Harcourt, Brace, 1955); and *Pablo Picasso, His Life and Times,* by Pierre Cabanne (New York: William Morrow, 1977). Guillaume Apollinaire also wrote of the episode (in somewhat turgid form) in a number of letters and essays.

98: ". . . by his wit and fancy . . ." *Charmed Circle,* by James R. Mellow (New York: Avon, 1975), p. 122.

99: "At about one o'clock . . ." Pieret's adventures on this and subsequent pages were detailed by him in *Paris-Journal,* Aug. 29, 1911.

100: ". . . very back of a cupboard." Olivier, *op. cit.,* p. 146.

100: ". . . gave them a thought." *Ibid.,* p. 146.

102: ". . . and its contents." *Ibid.,* p. 147.

103: ". . . to my destruction." Shattuck, *op. cit.,* p. 213.

103: ". . . avoid being deported." Cabanne, *op. cit.,* p. 145.

104: ". . . their childish grief." Olivier, *op. cit.,* p. 149.

104: ". . . off the scent." *Ibid.,* p. 150.

107: When he opened his door . . . *et seq.* The official report on the interview between Perugia and Inspector Brunet, made available to me at the Paris Prefecture, was dated Nov. 26, 1911.

PART FOUR: The Rift

114: ". . . of unsurpassed quality." Morgan's taste—and acquisitions—are legendary in the art world. The quote is from *The Proud Possessors,* by Aline B. Saarinen (New York: Random House, 1958), p. 57. Much other material on him can be found in *Merchants and Masterpieces,* by Calvin Tomkins (New York: E. P. Dutton, 1970).

116: "One feels a certain malaise . . ." *et seq. Mona Lisa, the Picture and the Myth,* by Roy McMullen (Boston: Houghton Mifflin, 1975), pp. 206–7. Sizeranne's original essay appeared in *Revue des Deux Mondes.*

119: With "infinite finesse" . . . "Why and How the Mona Lisa Was Stolen," by Karl Decker, *Saturday Evening Post,* June 25, 1932, p. 91.

119: ". . . an expert appraisal." *The Fabulous Frauds,* by Lawrence Jeppson (New York: Weybright and Talley, 1970), p. 46.

120: ". . . most of it was smuggled." Norton Simon's frank comment is noted by Karl E. Meyer, *The Plundered Past* (New York: Atheneum, 1977), photo caption following p. 100.

120: The market for stolen art . . . *et seq.* Information on missing works of art came largely from the private I.F.A.R. report, *op. cit.*; also *The Art Crisis,* by Bonnie Burnham (New York: St. Martin's, 1975); and Meyer, *op. cit.,* Appendix A, Table 3.

121: ". . . powerless to correct it." *Citizen Hearst,* by W. A. Swanberg (New York: Bantam edition, 1963), p. 551.

122: . . . handed over $300,000. The precise amount obtained from each victim has been reported by Jeppson (*op. cit.,* p. 46). It is also specified in *The Book of Lists,* by Wallechinsky and Wallace (New York: Bantam edition, 1977), p. 191.

128: During those long months . . . *et seq.* Regarding Perugia's growing rebellion, Curtis D. MacDougall in his book *Hoaxes* (New York: Dover, 1940) refers to the psychological phenomena "the incentive to believe." In Vincenzo's case, this incentive seems to have been concocted of disillusionment, vanity and greed. Any notions that the carpenter might have been acting alone are dispelled by the fact that he kept the portrait hidden for *well over two years.* Perugia's wages at that time averaged eight francs per day (about two dollars)—and he had various periods of unemployment. Given his precarious financial situation, it is most unlikely that he would wait idly *unless* he had been subsidized, which was of course the case. For the first year or so, Perugia fully expected orders from his chief, and it was Valfierno's neglect which triggered the simple man's resentment and incipient fantasies.

PART FIVE: The Recovery

PAGE

134: Alfredo Geri . . . *et seq.* Source material for this section came mostly from contemporary newspaper and courtroom files, made available to me at the Biblioteca Nazionale in Florence. Extensive newspaper coverage was provided by Florence's *La Nazione* and Rome's *La Tribuna* and *Corriere della Sera.* Additional details are from news accounts in Paris, London and New York, as noted. For background and local color, I am indebted to *The Stones of Florence,* by Mary McCarthy (New York: Harcourt, Brace & World, 1963).

134:   ". . . had been stolen from Italy." *The Art Stealers,* by Milton
Esterow (New York: Macmillan, 1973), p. 155.

138:   ". . . patrimony of Florence." *Ibid.,* p. 157.

138:   ". . . the painting was authentic." *Ibid.,* p. 157.

142:   "I have rendered . . ." Interview with Perugia in *La Nazione,*
Dec. 13, 1913, under the heading "PERUGIA IN THE MURATE."

144:   Professor Grassi's grandson . . . *et seq.* Interview with Marco
Grassi, New York, February 1979.

157:   Everyone was in a quandary . . . *et seq.* Comments by art experts as to the true value of the *Mona Lisa* were reported in *The
New York Times* on Jan. 25, 1914.

157:   ". . . ten percent of the inestimable." McMullen, *op. cit.,* p. 214.
An interesting sidelight to this involves the *Mona Lisa's* journey
to the U.S. in 1963. At that time, according to *The Guinness Book
of World Records* (New York: Bantam edition, 1971), p. 160, the
portrait was assessed for insurance reasons for the staggering sum
of $100 million. However the premium costs proved astronomic,
and the funds were used instead for better, stronger security.

158:   ". . . between reality and fantasy." *A General Introduction to
Psychoanalysis,* by Sigmund Freud (Garden City, N.Y.: Doubleday,
1943), p. 321.

161:   The court records . . . *et seq. La Nazione* is Florence's newspaper of record, and its yellowed pages provided most of the courtroom transcripts relating to Perugia's trial. These transcripts indicate that Vincenzo, who had had six months in which to consolidate
his version of the crime, put up a stubborn, effective defense. As
noted in the text, the Italian courts more or less "went through
the motions," and there was no real attempt to investigate the
fingerprint fiasco, the roles of Séguenot and the Lancelottis, or
other tangled areas.

170:   ". . . importance of it." Esterow, *op. cit.,* p. 177.

PART SIX: The Riddle

PAGE

175:   The entertainers sang: *Mona Lisa, the Picture and the Myth,*
by Roy McMullen (Boston: Houghton Mifflin, 1975), p. 211.

175:   ". . . like a band of . . ." *The Proud Tower,* by Barbara W.
Tuchman (New York: Bantam edition, 1967), foreword, p. xv.

176: No other painting . . . *et seq.* Decoding the *Gioconda* requires knowledge of the portrait's history as well as the life of Leonardo. Helpful sources included *Lives of the Artists,* by Giorgio Vasari (London: Penguin edition, 1965); *Léonard de Vinci,* by Marcel Brion (Paris: Éditions Somogy, 1954); *The Life, Times and Art of Leonardo,* edited by Enzo Orlandi (New York: Crescent, 1965); *Leonardo da Vinci,* by Kenneth Clark (London: Penguin edition, 1967); *La Joconde,* by René Huyghe (Fribourg, Switz.: Office du Livre, 1974); *The Renaissance,* by Walter Pater (Chicago: Academy Press, 1977); and *The Hidden Leonardo,* by Marco Rosci (Chicago: Rand McNally, 1977); as well as the writings of Carlo Pedretti, Bernard Berenson and Madeleine Hours. Mention must also be made of *Leonardo da Vinci and a Memory of His Childhood,* by Sigmund Freud (New York: W. W. Norton, 1964).

176: ". . . of the early 1500's." McMullen, *op. cit.,* p. 27.

176: ". . . all of them most perfect . . ." Clark, *op. cit.,* p. 157.

177: "For Francesco del Giocondo . . ." This and the quotation following it are from Vasari, *op. cit.,* p. 266.

178: ". . . an obscure Florentine citizen?" Clark, *op. cit.,* p. 112.

182: ". . . to the gross total." "Why and How the Mona Lisa Was Stolen," by Karl Decker, *Saturday Evening Post,* June 25, 1932, p. 91.

182: ". . . around her in circles." Schneider's comment reported by Guy Isnard in his *Faux et imitations dans l'art* (Paris: Librairie Arthème Fayard, 1959), p. 216.

184: The next bombshell . . . Jack Dean's curious story appeared in full in *The Sunday Express* of London on Aug. 6, 1933.

186: "In the last thirty years . . ." Interviews with Madeleine Hours and Lola Faillant-Dumas, Musée du Louvre, June 1979.

187: "No doubt the *Mona Lisa* . . ." Interview with Bonnie Burnham, International Foundation for Art Research, New York, April 1979.

188: "Another common practise . . ." *The Art Crisis,* by Bonnie Burnham (New York: St. Martin's, 1975), p. 149.

188: "At least a dozen . . ." Essay by J. V. Noble, *Macropaedia Britannica* (1974), Vol. 2, p. 91.

190: ". . . through the celebrated smile." *Self-Portrait with Donors,* by John Walker (Boston: Little, Brown, 1974), p. 63.

191: "With strong changes . . ." Interview with Michael Varese, Long Island, March 1980.

195: "the double mystery . . ." *et seq.* Isnard, *op. cit.,* p. 219.

198: "I remember very well . . ." This interview with Professor Nicodemi appeared in Milan's *Domenica del Corriere,* March 4, 1962. At that time there was a burst of interest in the Hekking portrait, with write-ups appearing in newspapers in Italy and southern France, but interest waned again after the elder Hekking's demise.

199: "After the publicity . . ." Interview with Patrice Hekking, Nice, June 1979.

200: He felt so strongly . . . *et seq.* Through the kindness of Mrs. Van Wemmel, I obtained a scarce copy of Henry Pulitzer's *Where Is the Mona Lisa?* (London: Pulitzer Press, 1966). Since this book outlines the complete "Pulitzer case," it proved to be a valuable source and I have quoted from it freely.

201: "The lady in question . . ." *Ibid.,* p. 9.

202: His former associate . . . *et seq.* Interview with Teresa Van Wemmel, New York, August 1979.

202: "I can only state . . ." Pulitzer, *op. cit.,* p. 97. In his book Pulitzer also espoused a "two *Mona Lisa*" theory, claiming that *his* was the genuine Gioconda portrait, and that the one in the Louvre was actually a painting of Costanza d'Avalos. His reasoning, however, is convoluted and unconvincing; Henry Pulitzer was on the right track but, in my opinion, was backing the wrong *Mona Lisa.*

203: In 1797 an elegant American . . . *et seq.* Information on the Vernon *Gioconda* came from personal interviews with the Vernon family, also from "Are There Two Mona Lisas?," by Emily Genauer, *This Week* magazine, *New York Herald Tribune,* May 7, 1950; "The Newport Mona Lisa," *Guaranty News,* December 1952; "Has New York An Authentic Mona Lisa?" by Joyce Kilmer, *New York Times,* Dec. 7, 1913; and "The Vernon Mona Lisa," Catalogue of the Otis Art Institute, Los Angeles, July–August 1964.

204: "The painting in my opinion . . ." Judson quoted by Wayne Long, Otis Art Institute, *op. cit.*

205: "Neither of the Vernons . . ." Genauer, *op. cit.,* p. 44.

206: . . . has clarified this, *et seq.* Interview with Agnes Mongan, Boston, April 1979.

207: "We just feel . . ." Interview with Suzanne Vernon Swick, New Jersey, January 1980.

208: . . . two architectural columns. The Raphael drawing is believed to be a study for a portrait of Maddalena Doni, an aristocratic young woman of Florence. Now in the Musée du Louvre, it unquestionably derives from the *original Mona Lisa.*

208: "To enjoy the *Mona Lisa* . . ." Bulletin on *Mona Lisa* by Rorimer and Rousseau, pub. by Metropolitan Museum of Art, February 1963.

209: When the picture . . . *et seq.* Interview with MM. Bollaërt and Verne in *La Comédie,* Paris, April 8, 1933.

210: "Set it for a moment . . ." Pater, *op. cit.,* p. 125.

213: ". . . give to portraits." Vasari, *op. cit.,* p. 266.

214: Establishing provenance . . . *et seq.* This is a highly sensitive area in the art world, and, as Agnes Mongan pointed out to me, a great distinction must be made between fraudulent claims and honest misattribution. Even the experts can make mistakes, and today most major galleries and auction houses take pains to protect themselves and their transactions. A recent catalogue of Sotheby Parke Bernet notes that all statements are qualified statements, and that the Galleries ". . . do not warrant and assume no risk, liability or responsibility for the authenticity of the authorship, the description, genuineness, attribution, provenance, period, culture, source, origin or condition of any property identified in this catalogue."

Similarly the brochure for Christie's auction house in New York City lists no fewer than *eleven* categories covering attribution of the paintings they offer for sale. Where an artist's name appears by itself in the catalogue, without any qualifiers, it is "In our opinion a work by the artist." The term "Attributed to ——" means that it is "In our qualified opinion a work of the period of the artist which may be in whole or part the work of the artist." The other categories run, in descending order, through "Circle of ——," "Studio or workshop of ——," "School of ——," "Manner of ——," "After ——"; also "Signed," "Bears signature," "Dated" and finally "Bears date," which means that the work "Is so dated and in our qualified opinion may have been executed at about that date." Such precautions are necessary, since the provenance of certain valuable art continues to be unclear, and misjudgments can result in losses running into hundreds of thousands of dollars.

214: "I remember very well . . ." Letter from Francis H. Taylor to Miss Mabel Clark, dated Feb. 18, 1952.

217: ". . . seventeen years old." *The Medici,* by Col. G. F. Young, (New York: Random House, 1930), p. 288.

219: ". . . an eloquent question." McMullen, *op. cit.,* p. 135.

219: ". . . recreate for himself." Clark, *op cit.,* p. 159.

220: ". . . of hostile superiority." McMullen, *op. cit.*, p. 219.

220: ". . . sensible-looking woman." Brezhnev quoted in *Painted Ladies*, by Muriel Segal (New York: Stein and Day, 1972), p. 54.

223: ". . . breathed his last." News item in *Le Petit Varois*, Toulon, dated Sept. 7, 1947.

Index